# PROFOUNDLY DISCON NECTED

A **TRUE** CONFESSION
FROM **MIKE ROWE**

ISBN 978-0-9914349-0-9

First Edition

Photographs courtesy of
Michael Segal Photography
Tom Roche Photo
Discovery Communications, Inc.

mikeroweWORKS Foundation
**PROFOUNDLYDISCONNECTED.COM**

# CONTENTS

**THIS BOOK WAS WRITTEN** in San Francisco, California, assembled in Peoria, Illinois, and inspired by a series of dirty adventures in all fifty states. The printing was made possible by inks manufactured in Cincinnati, Ohio. The paper in question was milled and sourced from Ticonderoga, New York and Luke, Maryland. The plates came from Dayton, Ohio, and the press chemicals were manufactured in Minneapolis, Minnesota. In other words, this book was made right here.

As for the actual typing, that was accomplished on a number of computers and word processors most likely manufactured in a variety of countries whose names I can neither spell nor pronounce. Welcome to the global economy.

# HOW MANY PEOPLE
# DOES IT TAKE TO PUBLISH
# A ONE-PAGE BOOK?

Too many to mention. Then again, this book is about saying thanks, so perhaps I'd better try.

**FIRST OF ALL,** *everyone ever featured on Dirty Jobs,* especially the entrepreneurs. Hard work is its own reward, and the willingness to get dirty is in short supply. But without entrepreneurial risk, no new job would ever get created. This book is about getting reconnected to work through a sense of personal appreciation. That means acknowledging the contributions of those who do the job, as well as those who create the job. Dirty entrepreneurs do both, and I hold each one of you in particular esteem.

*Every fan of Dirty Jobs,* especially those who watched at the beginning. Years ago, on the *Dirty Jobs* message board, a viewer asked me what it was like to work for the Discovery Channel. I replied that, even though they paid me, I didn't really work for Discovery—I worked for you. I still believe that. In my business, employers come and go, but in the end, we all work for the viewer or the customer. And that was really the biggest lesson from *Dirty Jobs.* You guys not only watched the show, you programmed it. You hosted it. And when I asked you to help me build mikeroweWORKS, you did that, too. For that, I'm profoundly grateful.

*Everyone who bought this fake book,* especially you. All proceeds go to the mikeroweWORKS Foundation to help reinvigorate the skilled trades in a variety of ways. In other words, this is a fundraiser, not *Moby Dick.* Thanks in advance for adjusting your expectations. (It's possible, of course, that this book was given to you. If that's the case, and you feel overwhelmed by the urge to support a worthy cause, please feel free to visit profoundlydisconnected.com and buy another copy. They make fantastic gifts.)

*Everyone at mikeroweWORKS*, especially Mary. mikeroweWORKS consists of several hardworking and cheerful do-gooders, but without Mary Sullivan at the helm, my Foundation, my career, my phone bill, and my personal economy would be too small to see with the naked eye. A recovering lawyer with a heart of gold, there is no harder worker, no wiser confidant, and no better-dressed partner than Mary Sullivan.

*Finally, I want to thank everyone at Caterpillar,* especially Sarah McDonnell.

As you may know, Caterpillar has done more to build America's infrastructure than any other company. They've also supported my efforts at mikeroweWORKS for years. But without Sarah, it wouldn't have happened.

Quick story. Years ago, I ran into a Cat technician who happened to be repairing a bulldozer on a construction site in Oklahoma. I asked him about his job, and he told me he loved it. Told me he was making nearly 100 grand a year. Told me Cat trained him for free and was always looking for people who weren't afraid to get their hands dirty. Said they had hundreds of openings.

I wound up flying over to Peoria to see if mikeroweWORKS could help call attention to some of the opportunities at Caterpillar. Met a woman named Sarah, who had nothing to do with tech recruitment but loved the idea of shining a light on great jobs that few people knew about. Through what can only be called dogged determination and sheer force of will, Sarah navigated me through the labyrinth of Cat Corporate and got me in front of the right people.

It only took her two years.

Today, Cat supports mikeroweWORKS, and I support Cat. But like every other successful partnership, it doesn't happen without people like Sarah. Hardheaded, good-natured, clear-thinking individuals who aren't afraid to step outside their comfort zones and make good things happen. Along with Lynette, and several other coconspirators, Sarah made this book a reality. Maybe next year, we'll do a whole chapter.

# FOREWORD

**I DON'T REMEMBER EXACTLY** when it happened, my transition from overprotective, fussy mother to world-weary, showbiz mom. I just know that when I turned on the television last month and saw my firstborn stripped to the waist and standing in fresh manure with his arm up the rear end of a bull, I didn't reach for a Valium. I merely shook my head and wondered for the hundredth time, how did this happen?

Ten years ago, my husband and I were enjoying the retirement couples dream about. We had sold the house and moved into a condominium. Our three sons were on their own, and we were enjoying the pleasures of life.

Then came *Dirty Jobs*

John and I sat in front of the TV that first Tuesday night like two wide-eyed children before the tree on Christmas morning. The record light flashed on the VCR, soda fizzed in our glasses, and the smell of buttered popcorn filled the den.

The opening credits appeared, and we smiled proudly as Mike's name appeared in the title of the little show he had created. It was good that Mike was paying tribute to those unsung heroes who do the jobs that make our lives comfortable. We were proud of him.

Suddenly, there he was, our son, sinking slowly in guano, surrounded by blackness and deadly fumes. As urine and other bodily fluids from millions of bats rained from above, a biologist warned Mike that the guano was filled with dermestid beetles committed to cleaning the flesh from his bones.

At the first commercial break, we turned to each other with our mouths open, the soda and popcorn untouched. When the phone rang, we knew before answering that it was Mike's frantic grandmother—but that's another story.

With each episode, even reruns, I am still filled with wonder. How does someone born into a middle-class home in the suburbs of Baltimore smile when he's sloshing through human waste or make jokes while he's straddling a 500-pound sow during artificial insemination? I not only marvel that I continue watching, I marvel that the adult on the screen is such a contrast to the child I nurtured.

I can still see that toddler in a high chair waving his hands after every bite and demanding, "Wash sticky fingers!"

When I learned how many millions of people worldwide watch the Discovery Channel's *Dirty Jobs*, I remembered a shy kid who dove beneath the kitchen table or made a beeline for the hall closet every time the doorbell rang.

"I don't want people to look at me," he would explain quietly. I used to lie awake nights envisioning my child's future as a pitiful recluse. Mike's amazing transformation came at Overlea High School.

"I got the lead in the senior play," he mentioned at dinner one evening. He said it in the same voice he might have used to say "Pass the potatoes."

"What's the matter?" Mike asked, as his father and I stared dumbly.

"Uh…, " I said. "Are we invited?"

"Sure. It's called *Oklahoma!* It's a musical." This was troubling, as Michael had never demonstrated the ability to carry a tune.

We huddled together in the school auditorium, chewing our fingernails, on opening night.

"Surely, they wouldn't let him do this if he weren't capable," my husband said.

We were dizzy from holding our breath by the time the curtain rose, and a rich, deep voice floated from the wings. "There's a bright golden haze on the meadow...."

We were dumbfounded. We sat at every performance, mesmerized, and before long were following our son's show-business career. There were community theater productions, barbershop quartets, and local TV commercials. When Mike joined the Baltimore Opera, two parents who didn't know the difference between *Sweeney Todd* and *The Barber of Seville* didn't miss a performance.

When Mike became a host on QVC in the early 1990s, we subscribed to cable TV. I set the alarm and sat in my pajamas drinking tea from 3 a.m. to 6 a.m. several times a week. My husband questioned my sanity. "Only a mother," he would say, rolling over in bed.

I watched my boy on national TV hawking merchandise he knew nothing about. I was horrified the night he burned his hand while cooking an omelet, and I cringed when he reached under the habit of a "musical nun doll," searching in vain for the winding mechanism. Once, he dozed off in front of millions of viewers while demonstrating bedding, leaving me to worry that he was sleep-deprived.

Years later, I would watch in horror as snakes and sharks sank their teeth into my son's body and cover my eyes as he washed windows from a bosun's chair 600 feet in the air. How I longed for the grave-yard shift at QVC.

I don't know what's around the corner for Mike, professionally, or for us, his most avid fans. I do know that I was especially proud of myself the night he was in a sewer with rats and roaches scampering over his body. I remained calm and didn't look away once. My son was unflappable as men in the sewer laughed at his effort to maintain a shred of dignity. It was then I realized the secret of

*Dirty Jobs*—if there was a joke to be made, it would always be on Mike, never at the expense of the people he worked with. I liked that!

I remembered a similar incident years earlier, a precursor perhaps of what was to come. Mike was a teenager, helping his brothers stack firewood on our patio, when he noticed a nest of young mice embedded in a log. He carried it to the backyard and tapped it hard against the ground, whereupon an entire litter of rodents emerged and immediately shot up his pants leg. I was nearly as frantic as Mike, who whooped and hollered, dancing around the yard.

"Somebody help him," I yelled.

No one did. Family and neighbors could only laugh hysterically as Mike dropped his jeans and pulled a mouse from his crotch. And then another. And then another after that. And though I never admitted it till now, I was laughing, too.

When *Dirty Jobs* finally finished its run last year, I was relieved but wondered what Mike would do next. He certainly had options. I voted for a sitcom, or Broadway, or maybe a sensible game show— something without snakes. Instead, Mike formed a Foundation that supports those industries that had been so good for *Dirty Jobs*. According to what I read in the papers (he still keeps us mostly in the dark), he's also awarding scholarships to kids and encouraging skilled labor in all its many forms.

Now I'm told he's written a book and asked me to write the foreword. Of course, I agreed, in spite of the fact he didn't tell me what it's about. For all I know, it's a pop-up. But if it is, I'm sure it will be worth reading. Even if it is only a single page.

*by **Peggy Rowe***

# PREFACE

## AUGUST, 2002

**WE'RE ANKLE-DEEP** in a river of raw sewage, sloshing single file through the bowels of San Francisco's subterranean wonderland. Our guide is a sewer inspector named Gene. Like me, Gene is dressed in canvas and rubber. He's sweating heavily, breathing through clenched teeth, and weighed down by a bucket of mortar that dangles from a rope looped around his neck. I carry a similar bucket in a similar fashion, while Branson creeps behind us with a television camera and a giant microphone on a long pole.

"Be careful, " says Gene. "It's slicker than snot through here. If you slip, it's better to fall backwards."

Gene's advice is excellent. Below us, the flotsam and jetsam of a million medicine cabinets bob and float on the chocolate-colored tide. Tampons and Q-Tips, diapers and dental floss, Kotex and Kleenex. The used condoms are especially ubiquitous. Unfurled, they cling to our hip-boots like colorful ornaments on limbless trees of black and shiny rubber. The smell cannot be described or overstated, but a GI Joe action figure, floating by on a giant turd, cannot be ignored.

"How much further?" I ask.

"Not far," says Gene. "A couple hundred yards. Maybe a little more."

As we descend deeper into the labyrinth, the tunnel begins to narrow, and the walls and ceiling begin to move. Roaches. Millions and millions of roaches are feasting on the permanent glaze of human excrement. Within moments, they spy our flickering head-lamps and rush over to investigate, covering us from head to toe like a living quilt. It's a page from Poe, a tableau from Dante, and a painting by Bosch, all combined and brought to life in a three-dimensional fresco of macrobiotic devastation. Branson quietly vomits into the effluvium but, God bless him, never stops rolling. I address the camera.

"As you can see, we're not alone down here. There's a surprise around every corner, and no telling what's waiting around the bend!"

"Try not to talk," says Gene, "unless it's really important. Nothing good happens down here when your mouth is open."

Again, Gene's advice is excellent but impossible to heed. I'm a television host. Talking is what I do. It's pretty much all I do. As I attempt to explain this, a watery jet of brown liquid explodes from a small hole inches above my head and splatters into the lens of Branson's camera. These holes are called "laterals," miniature tunnels that link up to a vast network of smaller pipes in the hills high above us and lead directly to thousands of individual commodes in the very best parts of town. In this way, the contents of a toilet in Nob Hill can gather a level of momentum far beyond that of a typical flush and enter our workspace at a velocity not often associated with human waste. Gene tosses me a methane detector.

"Here. Put this around your neck. If it goes off, run for your life."

We push on. Through the sewage. Through the stench. Through the roaches. A hundred yards later—or maybe a little more—we come to a crossroads.

"Here's the problem," says Gene. "This whole area needs to be redone." Gene wipes a few hundred roaches away from the ceiling and reveals a dozen or so bricks in the supporting arch in various stages of disintegration. As Gene gets busy digging them out, I look once again toward the camera, determined to inform the viewer with some fascinating facts about the sewers of San Francisco. At which point, my cohost appears.

He's about the size of a shoebox, with a tail like a riding crop. He may have crept up behind me, as rats often do, or he may have emerged from the lateral just above my head. Either way, he lands on my back with a moist and heavy thud. Then he's on my shoulder, reeking of urine and squealing loudly into my ear. I respond with some squeals of my own. He then tumbles into my crotch, enters the gap at the top of my my hip-boot, and begins to claw his way down my innermost thigh.

Naturally, I leap off my feet, smash my head into the four-foot ceiling, and fall forward into the sewage. The rat bolts from my boot. Roaches cascade from above. Branson vomits. I gag. Gene laughs.

"Hey, Mike, when you're done playing with the wildlife, come on over here and hand me that trowel. I could use an extra pair of hands."

I push myself up from the sludge and spit something out of my mouth. I try to recall the difference between Hepatitis A and B. Not that it matters. I have surely contracted both. Then I hand Gene the trowel and ask him how else I could be of service.

"Well, you could mix up another batch of mortar. I don't know about you, but I'd like to get out of here before people start coming home and taking showers."

For the first time, I really look at Gene. I look at what he's doing. I look at where he's doing it. And I try to imagine doing it every single day.

"Tell me they pay you a fortune," I say. "Tell me you're rolling in the dough." Gene hammers the chisel deep into the rotten mortar and starts to pry the old brick free.

"I wouldn't call it a fortune," he says, "but I'm doing pretty well."

"Yeah? How about the stink?" I ask. "Do you ever get used to it?"

"You can get used to anything," he says. "After a while, it smells like money."

The day wears on. Gene and I chat while we work. I learn some things about masonry. I learn some things about sewers. We share a few laughs. Then my methane alarm starts to beep, and we all run for our lives.

———

**LATER THAT EVENING,** after a series of hot showers and cold beers, I went back to my cubicle at CBS and took a look at the footage. I was not optimistic. My boss at *Evening Magazine* had allowed me to shoot an experimental segment called "Somebody's Gotta Do It." I had pitched the idea as a tribute to hardworking people who never get any credit for doing what they do. Gene certainly fit the bill, but I had no idea if the footage was even usable. The camera angles were impossible, the light was insufficient, and the day had been cut short by a wave of toxic gas. But I was wrong.

The footage was magnificent. In spite of all his vomiting, Branson had captured some really amazing stuff. The roaches looked like aliens, the sewage looked like toxic sludge, and everything else was beautifully and delightfully disgusting. Aside from the smell, it was exactly as I remembered it. The only problem was me. I was trying too hard. I was talking too much. Basically, I was acting like a *Host*, which is what I'd been doing most of my career. But down there in the sewer—surrounded by all that genuine reality—it felt fake.

Then, the rat materialized. I still couldn't tell where he came from, but watching his movements in slow motion revealed an obvious agenda and a route that now appeared predetermined. From my back to my shoulder in a twinkling. A deliberate pause, followed by a screech directly into my ear. Then another one. (What was he trying to say?) Then, a swan dive into my lap and a quick foray down my boot. I knew what came next, but watching it unfold was a weird mix of funny and horrifying. One moment, I was doing a bad impersonation of a local reporter. A second later, I was face-down in human feces, squealing like a ten-pound baby girl. I sat at my desk, transfixed. It was a rat intervention. And I couldn't stop watching it.

From that moment on, I forgot about the camera and focused on helping Gene. Turns out, he knew all there was to know about sewers (duh), and hearing him talk was a hell of a lot more interesting than listening to me spit out a bunch of facts I'd memorized the night before. But there was something else. Watching us work side by side, I saw that Gene's skill and knowledge were actually magnified by the absence of my own. This was humbling. Nobody likes to look incompetent, especially on television. But it was also real. And as I watched the novice learn from the expert, I saw the thing I had been trying to capture all along. I saw an authentic tribute to hard work. That's when it hit me: "Somebody's Gotta Do It" didn't need a host—it needed an apprentice.

Aristotle called these moments of profound realization "peripeteia," the part of a Greek tragedy when the hero realizes something that makes him see the world in a totally different way. (Hey, guess what, Oedipus—your wife is also your mother. Surprise!) I'd been hosting TV shows for nearly twenty years, and I was pretty good at it. But sitting there at my desk, seeing the evidence with my own eyes, I had a peripeteia of my own. I realized that I was done with hosting. I would no longer pretend to know things I didn't. I would no longer read from teleprompters and recite someone else's copy. From then on, I would let the worker be the expert. I would become a "perpetual apprentice."

A few months later, "Somebody's Gotta Do It" won an Emmy. A few months after that, I quit my job at CBS. And a few months after that, "Somebody's Gotta Do It" became *Dirty Jobs with Mike Rowe.*

As lessons go, that was a big one, but not the biggest. Because somewhere along the weird trajectory of my callow career, I had lost my connection to honest work. I was no longer mindful of the miracle of modern plumbing, or food production, or domestic manufacturing, or cheap electricity. Not because I didn't care about such things. But because I no longer had a personal relationship with the people who provided them.

*Dirty Jobs* changed all that. What began with a brief baptism in the sewers of San Francisco turned into an eight-year course in Peripeteia, with a minor in Humility, and three hundred mandatory field trips. Eventually, I got reconnected with work by getting to know hundreds of Americans who allowed me to walk a mile in their shoes. Granted, sometimes the walk was a crawl. Sometimes the road was a tunnel. And sometimes the shoes were hip-boots. But the journey was worth taking. And from the start, I was determined to see where the tunnel might lead.

"We've got millions of people looking for work and millions of jobs that nobody wants. College graduates are a trillion dollars in debt and struggling to find employment in their field of study. Meanwhile, 88 percent of all the available jobs don't require a four-year degree. They require specific training. So what do we do? We push a four-year degree like it's some sort of a Golden Ticket. We remove vocational education from high schools at the time we need it most. We're lending money we don't have to kids who can't pay it back, educating them for jobs that no longer exist. I'm no expert, but I'd say that's profoundly disconnected."

— **Mike Rowe,** to Bill Maher on *Real Time*

"How do you explain three million jobs that nobody seems to want? Well, if you're a conservative, you blame lazy workers and entitlement programs. If you're a liberal, you blame low wages and greedy employers. If you're a moderate, you blame a lack of training. Personally, I think they all miss the point. Because the Skills Gap is not a polemic. It's not even a problem. The Skills Gap is a symptom of what we value as a society. And right now we don't value hard work. We don't value skilled labor. We don't value alternative education. We didn't just 'wind up here.' We put ourselves here."

— **Mike Rowe,** to Glenn Beck on *TheBlaze*

"Remember Rosie the Riveter? When it comes to work, we used to have American Icons. Now we have American Idols. Is it any wonder no one wants to pick up a wrench?"

— **Mike Rowe,** to Oprah Winfrey on *Oprah*

"I've got mud in my shorts. At least I hope it's mud."

– **Mike Rowe,** to himself on *Dirty Jobs*

# INTRODUCTION

**OVER THE YEARS**, I've been flattered with a number of requests to write a book. Most of that encouragement has come from fans who have urged me to publish a collection of amusing stories and essays about my adventures on *Dirty Jobs*. That's a book I've been writing for years, and one day I hope you'll read it. Well, today is not that day. And this is not that book.

In fact, this really isn't a book at all. *Profoundly Disconnected— A True Confession from Mike Rowe* has only one paragraph.[01] Many of the pages are blank.[02] And the pages with actual writing are mostly reprints of articles I wrote and published elsewhere.[03] Nevertheless, this fake book has a real purpose, and according to Wikipedia, I'm supposed to spell that out for you in the Introduction. So here it is.

The purpose of this book is to help close America's Skills Gap and reinvigorate alternative education. I want to make more people aware that millions of worthwhile jobs are waiting to be filled. In this book, I attempt to do that by acknowledging my own dependency on a skilled workforce and challenging the reader to do the same.

That's it.

It's difficult to talk about big ideas without sounding like a blowhard or to be lighthearted without sounding glib. But for what it's worth, I really do believe that the time has come to broaden the conversation. The fact that three million available jobs can exist alongside record-high unemployment is proof positive that something is broken. I have no idea how to fix it, but I'm convinced the solution has to start with a new appreciation for hard work. America needs to reconsider the definition of a "good job." Likewise, a "good education." We've developed some stigmas and stereotypes around certain types of work and certain forms of learning. I think those stigmas have infected a whole generation and dissuaded millions of people from exploring lots of legitimate careers. Somehow, we've got to turn that around.

My theory is pretty simple. If more people understood the impact of skilled labor in their own lives, I believe those stigmas would vanish, and the Skills Gap would begin to close. Not right away. But over time, a heightened level of collective appreciation for hard work would change the way people look at lots of important jobs that are currently unloved, unwanted, and waiting to be filled.

Anyway, my confession is short, but 100 percent genuine. It speaks to my personal dependence on a skilled workforce, and it's my sincere hope that you'll find yourself in violent agreement with every single word. If you are, your mission is simple—buy this book, cosign it in the space provided, and leave it lying around in a place that might stimulate conversation with friends and coworkers.

If you don't agree, or if you feel skeptical about purchasing a fake book with just one official paragraph and lots of blank pages, I completely understand. But do me a favor. Buy it anyway. All proceeds go to the mikeroweWORKS Foundation. We're totally nonprofit, we're supporting the trades in a variety of meaningful ways, and we're awarding millions of dollars in work ethic scholarships.[04] In other words, think of this book like a box of Girl Scout cookies. You don't have to eat them to feel good about buying them.

Of course, my theory could be completely wrong. It certainly wouldn't be the first time I was both totally positive and completely mistaken about something terribly important. But either way, there's no danger in acknowledging our reliance on the work of others. Doing so led me to the first job I ever really cared about and a whole new identity. For me, confession was good for the soul. Maybe it's also good for the country?

*Mike*

San Francisco, 2014

**01** – Unlike traditional publications with multiple chapters and thousands of sentences, this book isn't bogged down with a lot of fluff. In various focus groups, most readers were able to complete the entire Confession in less than twenty seconds, freeing up hours of extra time for thoughtful contemplation or getting back to whatever it was they were doing before we sucked them into a focus group. Other advantages of owning a book with just one paragraph include the ability to read the entire thing before any money changes hands, which I encourage you to do right now. Doing so will take less time than the paragraph you're about to finish and eliminate any possibility of buyer's remorse. Although, as I explained earlier, disliking this book is a poor reason not to buy it.

**02** – This book contains a bunch of blank pages. They exist primarily to keep the front and back covers from touching and provide a little structural integrity to what would otherwise be a very skinny manuscript. They're also handy for note-taking and doodling, giving *Profoundly Disconnected* an element of functionality absent in most other books. However, our focus group was convinced that a bunch of blank pages was meant to symbolize something relevant to the subject at hand, and some of their assumptions are worth mentioning.

One participant saw the blank pages as a reflection of nearly three million jobs that nobody seems to want. Another likened an empty page to the actual value of a college diploma that's become too costly to purchase and too useless to leverage in today's job market. My own mother, somewhat cruelly, suggested that a book full of blank pages was not at all metaphorical, but rather "the inevitable and literal expression of an author with no actual qualifications who attempts to write about an issue of national importance."

Personally, if I were to try to look beyond their true purpose, I might suggest that this many blank pages indicates a conspicuous lack of new information on America's widening Skills Gap. The truth is, lots of respected economists and bona fide experts have written extensively about our country's dysfunctional relationship with work and education. Unfortunately, no one reads those books because they're long and boring. As opposed to this one, which is merely short and personal.

**03** – The Appendix contains a few previously published articles I've written over the years. Though relevant to the subject at hand, and wildly entertaining in their own way, please feel no pressure to read them. They're only here to provide a little context for those of you unfamiliar with mikeroweWORKS, and the quixotic mission that began twelve years ago in the sewers of San Francisco.

**04** – For more information on mikeroweWORKS, and how this book came about, check out the Afterword.

**THIS BOOK IS DEDICATED** to the Sewers of San Francisco, the men who keep them working, and the rat who made it real.

# MY CONFESSION | 01

**I AM AN ADDICT.** I am addicted to smooth roads, hot water, and indoor plumbing. I am a slave to sturdy foundations and affordable energy. I depend on others to grow my food, and I rely on people I've never met to keep the lights on. I am enamored of civilized life and totally reliant upon the hardworking men and women who provide it. I understand that without these people—without their skills and work ethic—polite society would crumble, and I would be in some very deep doo-doo.

*Mike Rowe*       Co-Signed: _____

Mike Rowe

# THE END

# AFTERWORD

**IN 2008, SIX YEARS AFTER** my sojourn into the Sewers of San Francisco, *Dirty Jobs* was the No. 1 show on Discovery, and I was firmly established as the dirtiest man on television. In other news, the U.S. economy was off the rails, and fourteen million people were out of work. Unemployment dominated the headlines, and according to America's top anchormen, all the jobs were gone.

On *Dirty Jobs,* though, the headlines were different. "Help Wanted" signs were everywhere. Welders, plumbers, drillers, carpenters, and mechanics all seemed to be in demand. In every state, business owners and entrepreneurs talked about the difficulty of finding people willing to learn a useful skill and work hard. They weren't talking about a lack of skilled workers -they were talking about a lack of people who were willing to reinvent themselves and do whatever it took to get the job done. There were reports of a Skills Gap, but this was something different. This was a willingness gap.

As the recession wore on, unemployment soared, and the Skills Gap widened. "Job Creation" was headline news, and politicians were using words like "stimulus" and "shovel-ready." And yet, there was very little press about the millions of jobs that no one seemed to want. Instead, there was lots of talk about the need for "good jobs." This was odd, because on *Dirty Jobs,* there was no such thing as a "bad" one.

From my perspective, the problem was obvious. Skilled labor had a PR problem. So, in the course of promoting a new season of *Dirty Jobs,* I didn't focus on exploding toilets and misadventures in animal husbandry. I talked instead about America's crumbling infrastructure, the widening Skills Gap, spiking unemployment, and the decline of domestic manufacturing. I shared what I was hearing from people I met on the show. And the more I talked about these things, the more I was asked to elaborate. So I kept talking.

I talked about the fact that a college degree was still considered superior to all other forms of "alternative" education, even with college debt approaching a trillion dollars and college graduates unemployed at record levels. I talked about the fact that 85 percent of all the available jobs no longer required a four-year degree. I talked about the value of apprenticeships and the free training that many companies provided to willing candidates. I talked about the absurdity of gutting vocational education from high schools at the time we needed it most. In short, I argued that three million shovel-ready jobs would be a tough sell to a country that no longer aspired to pick up a shovel. It seemed to me that America was losing its collective appreciation for hard work, in much the same way that I had. And I started to wonder aloud what might happen to a society so disconnected from something so fundamental.

One day, I got a letter from a fan who saw me on Leno and heard me ranting about everything in the previous paragraph. The fan agreed with my assessment, but asked, "Are you ever going to do anything besides talk about it?" It was a fair question. So I asked the fans of *Dirty Jobs* to help me assemble an online Trade Resource Center where people could find apprenticeship opportunities and training programs all in one place. I called it mikeroweWORKS, and we launched it on Labor Day of 2008. Over the next five years, mikeroweWORKS grew into a foundation, a scholarship fund, and most importantly, a PR campaign for skilled labor and alternative education. Our goals, however, haven't changed: Keep people mindful of the fact that a great education does not require an expensive, four-year degree and remind as many people as often as possible that lots of genuine opportunities still exist for those who aren't afraid to learn a useful skill and work their butts off.

Today, mikeroweWORKS is partnered with a number of companies and organizations around the issue of technical recruitment. We've awarded hundreds of work ethic scholarships and done all sorts of unorthodox things to keep the conversation going. This book is another one.

# A BUNCH OF BLANK PAGES

———

# A BUNCH OF BLANK PAGES

# A BUNCH OF BLANK PAGES

# A BUNCH OF BLANK PAGES

# PROFOUNDLY DISCONNECTED

# A BUNCH OF BLANK PAGES

PROFOUNDLY DISCONNECTED

# A BUNCH OF BLANK PAGES

# A BUNCH OF BLANK PAGES

# A BUNCH OF BLANK PAGES

PROFOUNDLY DISCONNECTED

# A BUNCH OF BLANK PAGES

# A BUNCH OF BLANK PAGES

# APPENDIX

**HERE'S A HOT MESS** of articles and ramblings that have appeared in various publications over the last decade. I thought they might give the curious reader a sense of how mikeroweWORKS took shape—and create the illusion of additional content, which, as you might imagine, is critical in a book with just one official page. In a sense, these appendices comprise the "long version" of my confession (see Chapter 01). Everything here has been distilled into the single paragraph that you've already read (and hopefully cosigned).

Here in the Appendix, you'll find a number of inconsistencies, contradictions, and redundancies. This is because I'm an inconsistent, contradictory, and redundant person trying to sort out my thoughts over the course of a long and smelly odyssey. Such is the price of making things up as you go.

# IT'S A DIRTY JOB, AND I LOVE IT!

*Forbes asked me to write a column a few years ago about my most memorable "dirty job." The truth is, I can't forget any of them. But the business of castrating a lamb orally still stands out. It was also one of the more controversial* Dirty Jobs *segments ever to air and formed the basis for a TED Talk that wound up getting a few million views.*

**I'VE BEEN THINKING** about the first time I castrated a lamb with my teeth. (It's a real job, I swear.) I was anxious, and judging by the sounds coming from the lamb, I wasn't the only one. He was propped up on the fence rail, pinned in place by a cheerful rancher named Albert, who was holding the animal's legs apart for my convenience. The blood in Albert's mustache was still wet from his demonstration moments before, and he spoke in a way that reminded me of the directions on a bottle of shampoo. "Grab scrotum. Cut tip. Expose testicles. Bend over. Bite down. Snap your head back. Spit testicles into bucket. Rinse and repeat."

It wasn't the first time I found myself cocking my head like an Irish Setter, wondering if I'd somehow misheard the instruction. (Spit testicles in bucket? Really?) I had assumed the same expression a few months earlier, when a jovial bridge worker explained that I would be walking up a skinny suspension cable 600 feet in the air to change a light bulb over the Straits of Mackinac. Likewise, when the happy-go-lucky Shark Suit Tester casually informed me that I would be leaping into the middle of a feeding frenzy to "field-test" the efficacy of his "bite-proof shark suit."

After four years and 200 dirty jobs, I'm no longer surprised by the variety of opportunities out there. What does surprise me is the fact that everybody I've met on this gig—with the possible exception of the lamb—seems to be having a ball.

It's true. People with dirty jobs are in on some sort of a joke. Maggot farmers are ecstatic. Leech wranglers are exultant. I've personally witnessed Lumberjacks and Roadkill Picker-Uppers whistling while they work. And don't even get me started on the crab-fishermen, spider-venom collectors, and chicken-sexers—they're having such a blast they've sworn off vacation. So why are people with dirty jobs having more fun than the rest of us?

The answer (aside from the fact that they're still employed) is because they are blissfully sheltered from the worst advice in the world. I refer, of course, to those preposterous platitudes lining the hallways of corporate America, extolling virtues like Teamwork, Determination, and Efficiency. You've seen them—saccharine-sweet pieces of schmaltzy sentiment, oozing down from snowcapped mountains, crashing waterfalls, and impossible rainbows. In particular, I'm thinking of a specific piece of nonsense that implores in earnest italics, to always, always...*Follow Your Passion!*

In the long history of inspirational pabulum, *"Follow Your Passion"* has got to be the worst. Even if this drivel were confined to the borders of the cheap plastic frames that typically surround it, I'd condemn the whole sentiment as dangerous, not because it's cliché, but because so many people believe it. Over and over, people love to talk about the passion that guided them to happiness. When I left high school—confused and unsure of everything—my guidance counselor assured me that it would all work out, if I could just muster the courage to follow my dreams. My Scoutmaster said to trust my gut. And my pastor advised me to listen to my heart. What a crock.

Why do we do this? Why do we tell our kids—and ourselves—that following some form of desire is the key to job satisfaction? If I've learned anything from this show, it's the folly of looking for a job that completely satisfies a "true purpose." In fact, the happiest people I've met over the last few years have not followed their passion at all— they have, instead, brought it with them.

I could give you pages of examples, but here are a few. Bob, the pig farmer in Vegas, who collects the uneaten food from casino buffets and feeds it to his swine, which now grow faster and more profitably than any other pigs on the planet; Matt, the dairy farmer in Connecticut, who realized his cows were producing more shit than milk and launched a successful line of biodegradable "flowerpots" made from pure poo; or John and Andy, a couple of entrepreneurs down in Florida, who retrieve wayward golf balls from alligator-infested water hazards and resell them on the Internet for big bucks.

These guys are passionate about what they do, but none of them aspired to the careers they now enjoy. None of them were guided by a burning desire to do a particular thing. What they did was step back from the crowd and watch carefully to see where everyone else was going. Then, they simply went the other way. They followed the available opportunities—not their passion—and built a balanced life around the willingness to do a job that nobody else wanted to.

Haven't we heard enough about successful people with "vision," who attribute their good fortune to some sublime "clarity of purpose"? Aren't you sick of triumphant tales that always start with a dream and end with a reward for the courageous hero who "stayed the course"?

Enough already. Wall Street needs some new role models—and I nominate the men and women of *Dirty Jobs*, beginning with Albert, who I'm quite certain is still grinning behind his bloody mustache.

Why? Because Albert knows that in a bear market you can't grab the bull by the horns—you can only grab the sheep by the scrotum and do the work at hand. That's right, boys. It's time to bend over, bite down, snap your head back, and spit.

It may not be the job you were dreaming of, but trust me, it is a job, and in these uncertain times, it could always be worse...you could be the lamb.

# 25 WAYS TO JUMP START
# THE AUTO INDUSTRY

*Back during the auto bailout,* Fast Company *asked me if I had any thoughts on how to fix Detroit. As the Ford guy, it seemed like the kind of question that could easily get me fired. But I answered it anyway and managed to keep my job.*

**REGARDING THE SPECIFIC ISSUES** facing the Big Three, I've got too little expertise and too much bias to weigh in with a straight face. (Trust me, that new F-150 really does kick ass.) However, after 200 dirty jobs and five years of unintended social anthropology, I do have a theory regarding our overall relationship with manufacturing and skilled labor. Here it is.

I believe the majority of people in this country are deeply disconnected from the Americans who still make our stuff. I think our fundamental relationship with work has dramatically shifted, and as a consequence, we are no longer sure what we really value.

Forty years ago, it was easy to "Buy American." Not just because our stuff was better than theirs. We bought American goods because we actually knew the people who were making the stuff in question. We knew them through a common relationship with work and a shared understanding of what it meant to have a "good job." In those days, of course, our economy was dominated and defined by manufacturing, and work had a recognizable, albeit dirty, face.

As consumers, we knew that face. In many cases, we were that face. It was a powerful and personal connection that tied us to the products we bought.

Today, that connection is gone. The seismic shift from Manufacturing to Financial Services has changed not only the composition of our Gross Domestic Product, it has changed our national mindset toward Work. We no longer celebrate the way things get made. We are more interested in the way things get bought. In this global economy, we focus only on the finished product, which makes the Americans who still make them largely invisible.

Tradesmen and Craftsmen, once depicted as role models, are now pointed to as examples of "alternative education." Popular portrayals of working people have slowly devolved into caricature and hyperbole. The Skilled Worker has become a distant drone, laboring away in some soon-to-be-closed factory, disconnected from any current definition of a "good job." Is it any wonder that Trade School enrollments are down? Can the state of our infrastructure really be that much of a surprise?

Much has been written about the drama between Management and Organized Labor, but the bigger struggle is our own dysfunctional relationship with Work. The symptoms may be in Detroit, but the problem is elsewhere. Actually, the problem is everywhere.

# A PRICK IN CONGRESS

*For the life of me, I can't remember where this first appeared. But it's here now. Another detailed answer to a fairly simple question about what compelled me to launch a website about hard work and skilled labor. And, more importantly, a rare opportunity to use the words "prick" and "Congress" in the same sentence.*

**A COUPLE OF YEARS AGO,** I went to Congress to see if anyone there was still up for an honest day's work. Turns out, there is. Dave Moralez has worked in Congress his whole career, but holds no elected office. He's a third-generation cattle rancher in Congress, Arizona, a tiny town in the Sonoran Desert. Dave is also a fan of *Dirty Jobs*, so when he wrote in to see if I'd like to help him transplant a cactus, I said "sure."

Dave Moralez looks like Work. He's deeply tanned and big all over, probably 300 pounds. He wears an enormous cowboy hat and a fat mustache that conceals a permanent grin. Unfortunately, there's not much to grin about in Congress these days. Another drought and a lousy economy have forced many ranchers there to rethink their business. Today, Dave pays the bills by selling his cacti, which grow in the mountains behind his house. "Yesterday I was rancher," he told me. "Today I'm a landscaper. Go figure."

My crew and I flew to Phoenix in early August. We spent the night in nearby Wickenberg, and headed over to the Moralez Ranch at the crack of dawn. Dave led me across the dusty yard to a big pick-up truck with a large iron cross built into the bed. Not standard. His sons, Dave Jr. and Daniel, were loading supplies—a tamping bar, three sledgehammers, two picks, a saw, an ax, some two-by-fours, a box of nails, and a case of water. There were also several long strips of indoor carpeting, skewered with dozens of cactus needles. Once loaded, Dave drove his truck toward a sunken arroyo that snaked through the back of his property and headed toward the hills. My crew and I followed in a tiny Hyundai, the last available rental at the airport and the only obvious choice for off-road desert adventure.

After twenty minutes of random twists and turns, Dave informed us via walkie-talkie that he was looking for a very specific cactus, near the top of very specific hill, somewhere off in the not-so-specific distance. Why his sights were set on one particular cactus was unclear, since we were driving past hundreds of identical candidates. They were all around us—towering spires of thorny defiance, poking out of the unforgiving terrain like enormous green lawn darts.

Eventually, we rounded a corner and came upon a bulldozer, parked at the base of a long, sloping ridge. We got out of our vehicles and walked over to the big yellow machine.

"Where did this come from?" I asked.

"I parked it here last night," Dave said. "We're gonna need it to build the road."

"I'm sorry—it sounded like you said...build a road?"

Dave grinned under his mustache. "I'm sorry, too, Mike. But we need to build a road to get to the cactus."

As is often the case with *Dirty Jobs,* there is no such thing as a singular task. So I wasn't shocked to learn that the business of transplanting a solitary cactus would require a few additional steps. I did not, however, anticipate the construction of a highway in the middle of the desert.

"Really," I said. "A road? Straight up a hill?"

"Relax," Dave said. "It's only a few hundred feet. And it's not like we're gonna pave it."

"Why not just yank the thing out and carry it down here to the truck?" I asked. This was maybe the funniest thing Dave Jr. had heard in a long time.

"What's so funny?" I asked. "You're telling me four guys can't carry one cactus down a hill?" Now Daniel joined his brother in a chorus of snorts and cackles, as Dave turned and pointed toward the top of the ridge.

There, backlit by the dawn's early light, I got my first look at our objective—a massive saguaro anchored into the hilltop a hundred yards away. If Central Casting were looking for America's Next Top Cactus, this was it. Fourteen feet tall, as wide around as a manhole cover, with two beefy arms curling up and out of its massive torso. It appeared to be giving me the finger.

"Holy crap," I muttered. "That's big."

"Big ain't the problem," Dave said. "That thing weighs two tons. That's 500 pounds a man. You really want to walk it down here?"

Sensing the rhetorical nature of his query, I responded with another question. "How old is that thing?"

"Well," Dave said, "based on its height, I'd say 200 years. Maybe more. It was probably standing right there when Jefferson was president."

Clearly, this was a cactus with a history, but as we trudged up the hill to give it a closer look, I realized that its resume did not include a "willingness to relocate." The base was completely encased in a slab of solid granite, and the needles that protruded from its leathery hide looked like punji sticks, patiently waiting for an opportunity to slide into something soft and fleshy.

"Wouldn't it be easier," I said, "to take a different one? Maybe one of those back there by the truck?" This got the brothers laughing again. "Dad doesn't do anything easy," Daniel said. "And besides, this is the one the customer wants."

I sighed and looked at Dave. "OK, then, what's the plan?"

Dave laid it out in simple terms. First we would build the road. Then we'd back the truck up the ridge and raise the iron cross from its rusty bed. Then, while the cactus was still in the ground, we'd secure it to the cross. There would be much hammering and swearing and, according to Dave, "a strong likelihood of bloodshed." Then the real work would begin. The trick was to remove the cactus with the roots completely intact, which meant digging well below the rocky surface. Once the roots came free, a hydraulic motor would lift the cross skyward, pulling the cactus up and out of its hole, into the bed of the pick-up, and off to greener pastures. "If we work fast," Dave said, "we can beat the heat and be out of here in three hours."

This time, I was the one who laughed. On *Dirty Jobs*, the only thing that takes three hours is three hours. And sure enough, three hours later, we were three hours behind. The heat was affecting our cameras and causing technical delays, and my own level of expertise on a vintage bulldozer wasn't helping.

By noon, the road was finally completed, but by the time we got the truck and the cross and the cactus properly situated, it was almost 2 p.m. and 110 degrees in the shade. I have no way of proving this, of course, as there was no shade to speak of. But the bloodshed Dave predicted is a matter of public record. I had been stabbed no less than a dozen times, trying to wrap strips of carpeting around the contact points between the cross and the cactus. For the record, the longer needles drew the most blood and gravitated toward the area under my fingernails. But the short ones were no less painful. They got below the skin and stayed there, working their way farther and farther in.

Anyway, the "real work," as Dave called it, finally commenced, and though it was four against one, I couldn't help but think the cactus had the advantage. Armed with a sledgehammer from the Civil War, I assumed a position on the downward slope and began to work on the granite surrounding the base. My first swing bounced off the rock like vulcanized rubber and sent the hammer flying straight back toward my head.

"You gotta swing it harder," Daniel said. "Like Dad." Dave stood across from me with an even larger mallet, which he swung with the ease and speed of a whiffle bat. Stone splintered. Dirt flew. Sweat poured. Dave Jr. stepped in with a pick, and Daniel stood by with a shovel to clear away the debris. I swung harder, and managed to chip away at ancient rock without knocking myself unconscious.

At first, the saguaro seemed indifferent; humoring our assault the way a horse tolerates a few flies. Then, as we began to expose the root system, the cactus began to fight back. No matter how careful I was, more needles of various sizes found their way into my shoulders and arms. Under Dave's mighty mallet, the rock slowly gave way and the hole grew deeper, but the cactus itself remained solidly anchored into the hill. It appeared to have a core of solid steel, with a giant magnet buried somewhere beneath it. The day dragged on. Blisters popped and oozed, sunscreen and sweat streamed into my eyes, and little silver dots danced in my periphery. Pausing for a refreshing bottle of boiling water, I marveled at the intractability of this primitive plant and quietly cursed my decision to accept Dave's invitation.

By 3 p.m., things had gotten personal. I had come to see the cactus as Excalibur and myself as a knight on a hopeless quest. When I broke my second pick handle of the day, Dave gave me the iron tamping bar with a chisel forged onto one end. It was far too hot to hold, but just right for cauterizing blisters, which is precisely what happened the second I grabbed it. By 4 p.m. Dave had employed his entire arsenal of tools to no avail. One of our cameras melted from the inside out, and I began to giggle for no apparent reason. A delirium was descending upon the whole scene, as the desert and everything in it conspired to drive us back to civilization. Meanwhile, the cactus stood firm.

I could spend pages walking you through every detail and every setback of "The Great *Dirty Jobs* Cactus Crucible." Maybe I should. People don't write about manual labor anymore—at least not the way they used to. And believe me, that afternoon in the desert would have brought the great ones back for an encore.

George Plimpton would have waxed poetic about the steady rhythm of sledgehammers, swinging in a Sisyphean counterpoint. Studs Terkel would have captured the closeness that manual labor can foster between fathers and sons. And Charles Kuralt would have turned a simple confrontation between a big man and a big plant into something even bigger. In their hands, Dave Moralez would have become Hemingway's "Old Man," plucked from the Sea and dropped into Eliot's Wasteland—an homage to all those scratching out a living in the rough terrain of their own metaphorical desert.

Anyway, that's a long answer to a short question. Sometime during my visit to Congress, I decided to look a little closer at our country's relationship with hard work, as well as my own. A few weeks later on Labor Day of 2008, I launched mikeroweWORKS. For the sake of a good story, I'd like to say that my decision occurred at the precise moment a two-ton cactus broke free of its 200-year-old address, but I really couldn't say for sure, since I was hallucinating at the time. The actual decision was probably made later that night, after we finally got that cactus out of the rock and onto the truck and into somebody's front lawn on the other side of town.

By then the sun had set, and I was too tired to drink the beer I'd been thinking about all day. (Almost.) Dave and I said our good-byes. He and his boys were headed home with great news. A casino in Vegas had just called with a rush order for 50 cacti. It was a month of steady work, and it would begin at 4:30 a.m. the next morning. The Moralezes were jubilant. I was dehydrated.

Back at the hotel, I liberated another Dos Equis from the minibar and jotted a few lines in my journal before passing out. Most of it is illegible, but the gist of it had to do with starting over. With reinvention. With what it must be like to find out that the path you've been on has come to an end and that the only way forward is on a road through the desert that you have to build yourself.

I fell asleep before I finished the beer, but my last conscious thought—as I pulled another needle from my sunburned shoulder—is still scribbled at the bottom of the page. "Hard work really is the thing that matters most. And in spite of all the pricks, there's still reason for hope—even in a place called Congress."

Happy Labor Day.

# THE FUTURE OF FARMING

*I'm a big fan of farmers and and a big supporter of the FFA. After speaking at their national convention in 2008, I was overwhelmed with requests to write about my views on the plight of the modern farmer. This piece was syndicated all over the place. Also of note: I first used the expression "profoundly disconnected" to describe our relationship with food. It's not so different than our relationship with work.*

**THE LAST TIME I WAS IN INDIANAPOLIS** was the summer of 2003. I remember it pretty well because I was still sulking about the Colts being moved there without my permission and not quite over their inglorious departure from my hometown of Baltimore twenty years earlier. My bitterness melted away, however, in nearby Plainfield at the National Chimney Sweep Training School, the site of my very first "dirty job." There, I was instructed in the fine art of "flue main-tenance" and engulfed in flames while attempting to extinguish a raging creosote fire from the top of a rickety demonstration plat-form. Things went downhill after that, and by the time I finally left town, I was unrecognizable, concealed under a thick layer of ash and soot, with no plans of ever returning to the Crossroads of America.

Of course, in those days I was unrecognizable on a daily basis. *Dirty Jobs* would not debut for another six months, and I had no reason to think that anyone would watch when it did. I was wrong about that, and I've been wrong about a great many things ever since. A few months ago, in fact—proving once again that my plans and my life have little in common—I returned to Indianapolis a lot cleaner, and a lot less anonymous, to deliver the keynote address at the 82nd National Convention of the Future Farmers of America (10/21/09).

For those of you who don't know, the FFA is an organization of 500,000 teenagers, most of whom look like they fell off the front of a Wheaties box. Wholesome, polite, and impossibly well-mannered, these are the kids you wish you had, diligently pursuing an adolescence of agricultural acumen. Unfortunately, I arrived at their annual convention with the same level of planning and forethought I brought on my last visit (i.e., none) and found myself pacing in the wings twenty minutes before my appearance, trying to arrange my thoughts into an "inspirational and G-rated message." Luckily, I happened to glance down at the "FFA Briefing Packet," recently handed to me by one of the organizers, and found some inspiration on page four.

"The FFA currently faces an image and perception problem. The previous name of the organization, 'Future Farmers of America,' lends itself to stereotyping by the public. The FFA faces a continuing battle to redefine itself against narrow perceptions of 'agriculture,' 'vocational' and 'farmers.' The name 'FFA' is now used instead of 'Future Farmers of America.'"

Incredible. Have we really become so disconnected from our food that farmers no longer wish to be called farmers? Apparently, yes. The FFA has determined that most Americans think of farmers like those actors in Colonial Williamsburg—smiling caricatures from *Hee Haw* and *Green Acres*, laboring quaintly in flannel and denim. From what I've seen, they're right. Over and over, I hear the same thing from farmers I've met on *Dirty Jobs*. Technical advances in modern agriculture now rival those of Silicon Valley, and today's farms are more efficient than ever, but no one seems to have gotten the memo. No one seems to care.

The question is "why?" and fifteen minutes later I was on stage, trying to provide a sensible answer to an audience of 55,000 future farmers who preferred to be called something else. I talked about the power of labeling and the dangers of typecasting, from Hollywood to Iowa. I relied upon my own mistakes and misperceptions to make my points (no shortage there) and told some stories about the education I've received in the course of shooting *Dirty Jobs*. I don't know that I was "inspirational" per se, but at the conclusion I was presented with some lovely parting gifts and left the stage to thunderous applause. In short, I had a blast and think the kids did as well.

Later that night, though, I discovered that there had also been some grown-ups in attendance. Some very serious grown-ups who run the kinds of organizations that actually put the food on our plates. People like Chad Gregory. Chad's a big shot with the United Egg Producers and claimed to have enjoyed my comments immensely. He is also convinced that the PR challenges facing groups like the FFA are not only real, but also critically relevant to anyone addicted to chewing and swallowing things.

Chad believes we have started down a slippery path that will forever change our nation's food supply. He talks passionately about the need for people to get educated about the realities of feeding a growing population and foresees a time when our country imports more food than it ships out. Chad says that without massive awareness and sweeping change, egg production in California will be all but eliminated by 2015 and that thanks to recent ballot initiatives, the process has already begun. He points to the confusion around the "free-range" issue and the power of groups like the Humane Society, which have taken their agenda to a whole new level. According to

Chad, one of their intended goals is now the elimination of all U.S. animal-based agriculture.

Chad wasn't alone. Walking around Indianapolis, I had dozens of similar encounters with a variety of people, all deeply concerned about the future of food production in this country and frustrated that the relevant issues have been framed by well-funded political organizations with very specific agendas. I listened to stories from agri-scientists about environmental groups fiercely opposed to biotechnical and chemical breakthroughs that would dramatically increase food production worldwide. I saw literature from PETA that likened beef production to "genocide." And a young farmer named Travis told me about a $1,200 fine levied by OSHA, because the bottom rung on one of his ladders was bent.

As I spoke with various farmers that evening, I realized that I had asked the wrong question. "Why?" is too easy. Obviously, today's farmers need a PR campaign because they are beset by an army of angry acronyms, each determined to change modern agriculture in a way that better reflects their particular worldview. The better question is "How?" How is it that 300 million Americans—all addicted to eating—have become disconnected from the people who grow our food? What new priorities have captured our shared concern?

The answer depends entirely upon whom you ask. PETA has one response; the Sierra Club has another. The Humane Society might see it differently than the EPA, and Greenpeace has a different reply than OSHA. Fair enough; it's a free country. But how did these organizations get so much power? Are their arguments really that compelling? Are their leaders really that charismatic? Are their members really that enlightened? Or has our prosperity created a toehold for ideas that would have simply died on the vine one or two generations ago?

Imagine the HSUS successfully closing down California egg production back in...1960. Or in the same year, imagine OSHA fining a family farm $1,200 for a bent ladder. Imagine telling hungry Americans decades ago that environmental policy would make it impossible to maximize food production. I'm not looking for a fight—really, I'm not. I understand that different things are important to different people, and I don't begrudge anyone's right to champion the issues that matter most to them. But what's more important than eating? What's more important than feeding a hungry planet and supporting the people who grow our food?

On *Dirty Jobs,* I'm no expert, and I'm even less of one here. But I have a theory, and it goes like this—all jobs rely on one of two industries: mining and agriculture. Every tangible thing our society needs is either pulled from the ground or grown from the ground. Without these fundamental industries, there would be no jobs of any kind. There would be no economy. Civilization begins with miners and farmers, and polite society is only possible when skilled workers transform those raw materials into something useful or edible.

I started mikeroweWORKS.com because I think we've become disconnected from that basic premise. I think we've simply forgotten about the underlying industries upon which all else depends and as a result, created for ourselves a vocational identity crisis. Our collective definition of a "good job" has evolved into something that no longer resembles Work, and that has detached us from a great many things, including our food and the people who provide it.

Could this be the root cause of the FFA's "perception problem"? Could our warped view of the modern farmer be just another symptom of our warped relationship with work in general? It's just a theory, but how else can we explain a country that marginalizes and stereotypes the very people we depend on most? From what I've seen, most people like farmers. Most people like food. The problem is Work. We've spent decades trying to distance ourselves from traditional notions of Work. And who embodies Work more than the American Farmer?

If Chad's right, U.S. animal agriculture is under siege, and we're well on our way to getting our eggs from China and our beef from Brazil. Perhaps this would please the Humane Society. Perhaps PETA would like to see those items removed from menus altogether, and that's fine. People often disagree about important matters, but without context, the bigger issue gets lost. This is our food supply we're talking about—not the size of a chicken's cage or the resistance to chemically enhanced soil. We already rely on the world for our energy. Do we really want to rely on them for our food as well?

I auditioned the other day for the voiceover on a TV commercial about the American Farmer. (Yeah, I still audition.) I don't recall the whole thing, but it started out like this: "Every year we demand more and more from our farmers. More food from less land. More food from less energy. More food from less labor. And every year our farmers deliver."

I believe that to be a true statement. I also believe that as a country we haven't made it easy for them. Two percent of our population provides the rest of us with all the food we need, and we behave as though it's our birthright. Like nothing we do can threaten the abundance. It seems to me that as a country we could do a better job of supporting the people who feed us. And we could start by acknowledging the incredible challenges facing the American Farmer.

But I digress.

All I really wanted to do was congratulate the FFA for their good work and thank them for inviting me back to Indianapolis. I spend a lot of time these days talking about the importance of getting dirty—mostly with white-collar workers who don't really know what I'm getting at, which is fine. Preaching to the choir doesn't do much but bore the choir, so I rarely take the opportunity to talk to groups who already "get it."

However, there is something to be said for occasionally finding yourself in the company of like-minded people. And every so often, if you can get your thoughts organized in time, it's fun to address the rafters and deliver a message that gets 50,000 enthusiastic future farmers to stand up and holler back with unbridled gusto.

Such were my last three days in Indianapolis. Good for the spirit, good for the ego, and far superior to crawling down a flaming chimney. Not that there's anything wrong with that....

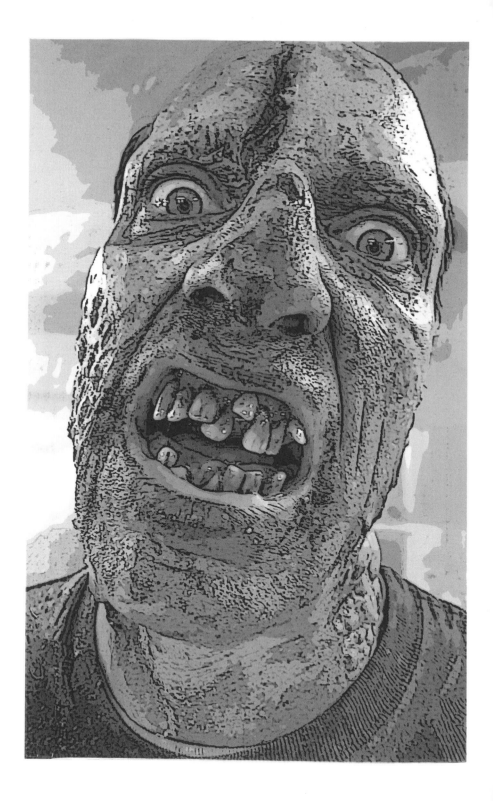

# IS THERE A ZOMBIE IN YOUR HOUSE?

*This is an edited version of a much longer piece I wrote for newspapers across Georgia in 2011. The Skills Gap down there is reaching crisis levels, and I was helping a campaign designed to impact recruitment in the construction industry. Given the success of The Walking Dead, and the advent of Halloween, I couldn't resist a zombie metaphor.*

**PSYCHOLOGICALLY,** the journey from TV host to brain-dead zombie is a fairly short one. Physically, though, the transformation requires time, skill, and a lot of hard work. I learned this firsthand from Toby Sells, a talented special-effects artist who turned me into a soulless corpse for an episode of *Dirty Jobs with Mike Rowe* back in 2007.

Toby plies his trade in a creepy little studio outside Atlanta. He studied his craft for years as an apprentice, practiced under the supervision of a seasoned professional, and worked his butt off getting very good at what he does. Then the world came to an end over on AMC, the zombie business blew up big time, and Toby got busy breathing new life into the walking dead. Today, he's still carving out his own pound of flesh from an industry that thousands are dying to get into.

Unfortunately, while millions of legitimate zombies are alive and well, the work ethic and apprentice model that put Toby Sells in business is now on a kind of deathwatch. And this Halloween, you'll see the results, as a whole new breed of trick-or-treaters knock on some very familiar doors.

But these "walkers" are looking for more than candy. They want dinner. And breakfast. And brunch. And car payments. And if you don't answer the door, they won't leave a bag of burning dog crap on your porch or wrap your shrubs in toilet paper. They'll just let themselves in with the spare key, raid your fridge, crash on your couch, and play *Call of Duty* and *Halo* until someone turns off the electricity. These are zombies of our own making. And they'll scare you shitless.

The facts are pretty simple, even if the numbers are big. A trillion dollars in student loans. Three million available jobs that don't require a four-year degree. And tens of thousands of unemployed college graduates moving back home, perfectly educated for jobs that no longer exist and completely untrained for those that do. It's a nightmare.

But really, how surprised should we be? We've gutted the technical trades from our high schools and consistently portrayed vocational education as something..."alternative." And yet, we still push a four-year degree like it's the best path for the most people. The result? A one-size-fits-all approach to education that all but guarantees the dysfunctional relationship with hard work and skilled labor we have today.

mikeroweWORKS is an attempt to turn that around. At its base, it's a PR campaign for alternative education. By the end of this year, we'll award around $3 million in work ethic scholarships to a small number of extraordinary trade schools, beginning with Tulsa Welding School and Midwest Technical Institute. These scholarships are designed to reward two things: the willingness to work hard and the desire to learn a useful trade.

In the near future, you may expect to see me interrupt your favorite TV programs (maybe even your favorite zombie drama) with short messages in support of this endeavor.

Thanks in advance for not fast-forwarding through them. But, if you must, you can support our efforts in a variety of other nontraditional ways at mikeroweWORKS.com.

Ultimately, closing the Skills Gap will only happen when the entire country starts to think differently about the definition of a "good job." This will come down to parents, teachers, pundits, Scoutmasters, clergy...anyone in a position to influence a kid who's trying to figure out what he's good at or what to do with the rest of her life. We need to change some fundamental stigmas and biases toward hard work and skilled labor, and that won't be pretty.

But, hey—if the zombie trade is booming, maybe there's hope for those industries that make civilized life possible for the living?

And maybe, with a little luck, we can keep the "walking dead" where they belong—on TV and out of our refrigerators.

Happy Halloween.

# BROWN BEFORE GREEN

*Alternatives are important not just in education, but to every major issue involving work and learning. On* Dirty Jobs, *I met a lot of people who had alternative ideas regarding the environment. Many farmers, for instance, worked hard at being good stewards of the Earth, but resented the pressure to conform with all things "green." I looked for an alternative color and thought brown might be a more palatable shade. We produced a* Dirty Jobs *special called "Brown Before Green" and ruffled a few feathers. This was one of the many articles that showed up around the premiere. A version of this first appeared in* Men's Health.

> **Editor:** *We asked Mike Rowe, host of the Discovery Channel's* Dirty Jobs, *for an interview. He declined, but agreed to chat with himself, one-on-one, in an L.A. hotel room. Here's what he had to say...to himself.*

*[M.R.:]* **Thanks for talking with me today. I'm a huge fan.** *[Mike Rowe:]* Likewise.

**People are calling *Dirty Jobs* the "greenest show on television." Does that surprise you?** Not really. Over half of the 175 jobs we've profiled in the last three years have a positive impact on the environment. Sooner or later, somebody was bound to notice.

**Why do you think it took so long?** Because I'm not trying to save the planet. I'm trying to profile people with dirty jobs. I had no idea the dirtiest jobs would turn out to be so environmentally friendly. It just so happens that the greenest people in the world are usually covered in dirt, or some other shade of brown.

**You're talking about garbage men and sewage workers?** Yeah, but I'm also talking about entrepreneurs. Like the guys in Florida who scuba dive for golf balls in alligator-infested water hazards and resell them online. Or the dairy farmer in New England who markets biodegradable flowerpots made from cow poo. Or the pig rancher in Las Vegas who collects tons of uneaten leftovers from casino buffets and feeds it to his hungry swine. We've become conditioned to equate "green" with "clean." That's just silly. Underneath all the dirt, the filthy people on my little show are greener than Al Gore in a cabbage patch.

**Is that what you meant when you told Larry King "Brown is the New Green"?** Actually, what I said was "Brown before Green." Like in the dictionary.

**So your position on the issue is alphabetical?** That's funny. Very few people who want to talk about the environment these days have a sense of humor.

**Why do you think that is?** Because the "Greens" have been busy scaring the crap out of us. Haven't you heard? "Your SUV is melting Greenland. Your hairspray put a hole in the ozone. Your kids are going to inherit a charcoal briquette."

**Well, the stakes are a little scary. Should we really be laughing about global warming?** No. But relying on fear and guilt to modify behavior ultimately leads to comedy. Like in my hardware store, where they tell me the plastic rake in Aisle 4 is "environmentally friendly" because it saves wood. Then, further down the same aisle, they promote a steel rake with a wooden handle as "environmentally friendly" because it uses a "renewable resource." What a crock. I still don't know the right answer to "plastic or paper?" Does anybody?

**You seem a little pissed.** I am. Look around this hotel room. Nice, right? Well, there's a sign in the bathroom that says, "If you really need fresh towels, leave the used ones on the floor." The sign is covered with little green raindrops with "sad faces" drawn into them. Ridiculous.

**Why is it ridiculous? What's wrong with saving water?** Well, doesn't saving water save the hotel money?

**Sure. What's wrong with that?** Nothing. But shouldn't I expect to see those savings passed on to me? I'm the one using the damp towel, right? Where's my rebate? Do you think I'll see an adjustment on my bill when I check out?

**Wow. I hadn't looked at it that way. You're smart.** Thank you. There's another sign just like it on my pillow, encouraging me to sleep in last night's sheets. And my favorite is on the back of my toilet. That one says, "It's Your Planet—Keep it Green!" What the hell does that even mean? What are they trying to tell me?

**When I was a kid, we had a sign in our bathroom that said, "If it's yellow let it mellow, if it's brown flush it down."** (Laughs) Now that was a sign. Clear, clever, and impossible to misinterpret. Do you think this hotel is asking me to save water by not flushing my pee?

**Sounds like it. Do you have a problem with that?** Not at all. Hell, I'll piss in the shower if it'll save me a few bucks. But at $500 a night, I don't need green raindrops with sad faces trying to influence the fate of my yellow urine. These are the same people who ask me to spend five dollars for a bottle of water—a plastic bottle no less. You have to laugh.

**So you're sympathetic to the cause, but critical of what exactly—the execution?** To be honest, I'm sick of green. I'm tired of being lectured by people who care more for the planet than the people on it. A lot of what gets characterized in the press as "environmental concern" strikes me as little more than a power grab, and anything that brings Hollywood and Washington this close together gives me the creeps. If we're talking about the importance of cleaning up after ourselves and leaving a light footprint, I'm all for it. But there are a lot of "inconvenient truths" in the environmental movement and a ton of manipulation. That leads to hypocrisy and opportunism. Mainly, though, I'm just appalled by their choice of color. I mean, seriously—green? What were they thinking?

**What's wrong with green?** Green is the color of money. The color of mold. Green is the shade of envy. Jealousy is the green-eyed monster. Never mind Mean Joe Greene. Or gangrene. Why base a movement geared to save the planet on such a hideous hue? Metaphors and imagery are powerful, and green stands for nothing good.

**Well, it's the color of spring, right? Symbolic of rebirth and renewal?** Big deal. Spring is only impressive because it follows winter. It sticks around for two months, brings rain and mosquitoes, then leaves abruptly. Spring year round would be a nightmare.

**Your position, then, is that the Green Movement would have been better off had it simply rallied behind a different color?** Any other color would have been preferable. Yellow would have been nice, since there is no life without the sun. Blue would have made sense, too, since life began in the oceans. But brown is far and away the best.

**Spell it out for me.** Brown is the color of dirt, and dirt is the color of Earth. Under the blue ocean, the green forest, and yellow sun, there is always brown—a combination of all the primary colors. Steadfast. Fundamental. Unglamorous. Our food grows in the brown. Our bodies return to the brown. Without brown, there is no growth. There is no green.

**You've put some thought into this.** I'm not done. The people I meet on *Dirty Jobs* would never describe themselves as "green," yet they do more to clean up our environment in the course of making a living than any celebrity ever will. If you were looking to launch an environmental awareness campaign that real people can relate to, I'd say "Get Down with Brown" and hire a plumber to act as spokesman.

**So you're not impressed with the efforts of people like Al Gore and Leo DiCaprio?** I'm not going to question anyone's agenda or motive. But I strongly suspect that millions of responsible Americans who see themselves as environmentally conscious have been turned off by the marketing of green and might feel uneasy about falling in line behind movie stars and politicians. Celebrities might generate awareness, but they divide as well as they unite. And as role models, they're just not relatable.

**Aren't you a celebrity?** Please. I'm on the cover of a *Men's Health* supplement. And I'm interviewing myself.

**Good point. I want to thank you for your time. You fascinate me. May I use your bathroom and buy a $5 water for the road?** The water's my treat. Just turn off the lights on your way out. And please, feel free to flush.

# SAFETY THIRD

*Just because the speed limit is 55 doesn't mean you should drive that fast when the road is covered with ice. That was the point of "Safety Third"—to challenge the idea that being in compliance was the same as being safe and to point out the complacency that often follows mandatory safety protocols.*

*Well, the "Safety Third" special on* Dirty Jobs *certainly got the conversation started. Hundreds of articles appeared all over the place. Some called for my head (ironically), and some were complimentary. One editorial in a highly respected safety publication nearly got me fired. But on the positive side, I think it made people more inclined to take as much responsibility as possible for their own well-being. Which was always the point. Here's my reply to the editor.*

**MIKE ROWE HERE,** *Dirty Jobs,* etc. I'm writing to thank you for your article in May's edition of ISHN and for sharing with your readers a few of my comments on workplace safety. Over the years, I've learned that some Safety Professionals do not always welcome criticism, especially from a smart-aleck TV Host. I don't blame them. No one likes to be second-guessed by a wise guy who needs a bath and has no credentials. Thanks for keeping an open mind and providing some context for my comments. Here's some additional background that

you're welcome to share with your readers, if you think it would be of interest.

The comments you attributed to me first appeared in a blog called "Safety Third," which I wrote for my website back in 2008. "Safety Third" told the stories of my various encounters with over-zealous Safety Officers. The first one I recall involved a very cranky gentleman who demanded I wear a harness while working on a scaffold that was maybe four feet off the ground. When I pointed out that the safety line attached to the harness was longer than the distance between the ground and me, he said, "Don't argue! Safety First!" Later that same week, a Safety Officer with the Department of Natural Resources interrupted our shoot to insist I put on a life jacket while installing a culvert in a run-off pond. The water in the pond was less than a foot deep. When I asked him to explain the need for a grown man to wear a life jacket in ten inches of water, he offered the same words of wisdom—"Safety First!"

I have never understood the point of ranking virtues and values in order of their importance. If Safety is First, what is Second? Or Fifth? Or Ninth? In the Boy Scouts, we used to say "Safety Always," which made a lot more sense to me. Safety Third became my default reply whenever someone acted as though my safety was their respon sibility. On *Dirty Jobs,* I met many such people. And for a while, I actually believed them.

From 2004 to 2008, the *Dirty Jobs* crew visited more hazardous sites than any other crew in the history of television, from crab boats to coal mines, from the very tops of the tallest bridges to crocodile-infested swamps. During that time we sat through close to a hundred mandatory safety briefings. We all became intimately familiar with all the basic protocol—lock out tag out, confined space, fall hazards, respiratory precautions, PPE, the endless checklists, etc., etc. Through it all, trained professionals were on hand to remind us (and our cameras) that our safety was their top priority.

For a while, it worked. We managed to deliver three seasons of *Dirty Jobs* with no accidents. Then things started to unravel. Stitches, broken bones, sprains, contusions, falls, a damaged eardrum, second- and third-degree burns, and many more near misses...it was weird. The job sites were no more dangerous than they'd always been, but the mishaps among my crew were skyrocketing. Then one day, a man was killed while we were shooting in a factory near Pittsburgh. He was crushed by the door on a giant coke oven. In the break room, where I was told of the accident, a large banner said, "We Care About Your Safety!" That got me thinking about things like unintended consequences and the dangers of confusing compliance with real safety.

I found a study on traffic accidents that claimed the most dangerous intersections were those with signs that told you when to walk and when to wait. Intersections with no such signs were statistically safer, apparently because people were more likely to look both ways before crossing the street if there was no blinking sign to tell them when it was safe to do so. According to the theory of Risk Compensation, people subconsciously maintain their own level of "risk equilibrium" by adjusting their behavior to reflect the changes in their surrounding environment. Thus, when the environment around us feels unsafe, we take fewer chances. And when that same environment feels safer, we take more chances. That got me wondering—if companies and Safety Professionals tell us over and over that our safety is their priority, wouldn't that tend to make us feel safer? And wouldn't that in turn, prompt us to take more risk, therefore making us...less safe?

I'm no expert, but I think that's exactly what happened to my crew and me. Over time, we had become convinced that someone else was more committed to our well-being than we were. We became complacent. We were crossing the street because the sign told us it was safe to do so. But we weren't looking both ways.

In 2009, Discovery agreed to air a one-hour special called *Safety Third.* On *Safety Third,* I talked candidly about mistakes we'd made on *Dirty Jobs,* and the unintended consequences of putting Safety First. I argued that many compulsory safety programs discouraged personal responsibility in favor of Legal Compliance. I asked viewers to consider all the amazing progress that would have never occurred had safety been valued above all else. (I also pointed out that if big companies really believed that Safety was First they would wrap their employees in bubble pack and send them home.) I concluded by saying that "Safety Third" was a lot more honest than "Safety First" but, ultimately, too important and too personal to be reduced to a platitude. But if we had to have one, my vote was for "Safety Always."

Well, hell. I might as well have suggested that we replace steel-toed boots in favor of flip-flops. Or outlaw hardhats. I got a nasty letter from OSHA and a flood of angry mail calling me a "bad role model." NASA was pissed. So were several Labor Unions and dozens of Fortune 500 companies who took exception to my "irreverent tone." I even got a snippy letter from PETA, though I'm still not sure why.

Safety Third had ruffled a lot of feathers, but I was thrilled by the response. I answered all the angry mail and went to speak personally to those organizations and companies who were most offended. For the most part, skeptics came to agree that the underlying concepts of "Safety Third"—common sense and personal responsibility—were still worth talking about and conceded that any resulting conversation which might lead to heightened awareness would ultimately be a good thing. Your piece, Dave, is now a part of that conversation, and I'm grateful.

As for the rest of your article, there is one thing I need to address directly. While it's true that I am "macho" far beyond the accepted definition, I am not, as you suggest, "America's number one blue-collar guy." I have no "blue collar bona fides" to offer and no permission to speak for anyone but me. It's important to be clear about that, because my opinions are not necessarily those of Discovery, Ford, Caterpillar, or anyone else with whom I may do business. In fact, I should thank all those companies for their patience with me, as many of my comments on this subject have been taken out of context and have no doubt caused some internal discomfort.

The truth is, "Safety Third" has caused me all sorts of headaches over the years, but I still think it's a conversation worth having. Everyday, workers fall through the cracks of a one-size-fits-all safety policy. Complacency is the real enemy, and I'm pretty sure the way to eliminate it will not involve more rules and more soothing assurances that an individual's safety is someone else's priority. Workers need to understand that being "in compliance" is not the same as being "out of danger." That's not going to happen by repeating the same dogma that's been out there for the last hundred years and forcing people to watch thirty-year-old safety films that would put a glass eye to sleep.

I realize that "Safety Third" sounds subversive and irreverent. It's supposed to. But it's not a call to completely dismantle accepted procedures and protocols. It's an attempt to improve upon them and generate a conversation around a topic that really does affect everyone; hopefully, a conversation that will lead to fewer injuries on the job. A few ruffled feathers seem a small price to pay.

— *Mike*

# YOUR HEADLINE, MY FACE

*The notion of "good jobs" versus "bad jobs" is central to the whole idea of a larger disconnect with honest work. It's annoying, and one night, it came to a head on Facebook. I found an article that posed the question, "Are Bad Jobs Good for the Economy and the People Who Do Them?" Next to the headline was the photo on the preceding page. My response was fueled by a small measure of righteous indignation and a slightly larger measure of sambuca.*

**HI STEVE,** Mike Rowe here, *Dirty Jobs*. Thanks to the necromancers over at Google, I've been alerted to your most recent Question of the Day: "Are Bad Jobs Good for the Economy and the People Who Work Them?" Immediately under your headline I noticed a photo of me, taken on the Mackinac Bridge while filming a segment on *Dirty Jobs*.

Given the juxtaposition of my face with your headline, a reasonable person might conclude that a "dirty job" and "bad job" are one and the same. This sentiment is not only inconsistent with my own view of hard work, it's completely at odds with the "*Dirty Jobs* Code of Conduct," a collection of life lessons painstakingly compiled from the men and women I've met on *Dirty Jobs*.

Over the years, the "*Dirty Jobs* Code of Conduct" has kept me from saying stupid things in the press. Today, it's used primarily to assist writers like you with the approved use of my name and likeness.

Obviously, you have never seen or heard of the *"Dirty Jobs* Code of Conduct," since most of your article violates every clause and restriction therein. I must therefore take a moment to assure your readers that the appearance of my face in such close proximity to your headline is in no way a personal affirmation that certain types of jobs are in fact "bad."

Here, then, are a few basic guidelines on the proper use of my name and likeness, pulled directly from the most current version of the DJCC. Since your question of the day is clearly not rhetorical, I'll attempt to answer it here, with a level of detail that could only occur on a cross-country flight with no movie, no crossword, and a dead Kindle.

———

*[Steve K.:]* **Most of us can tell a story about a job from hell somewhere in our past. There's the first job, the one we took because our parents said, "You can't hang around the house all summer long." Maybe it was at a fast-food place or in a retail outlet.** *[Mike Rowe:]* First of all, Steve, the *"Dirty Jobs* Code of Conduct" contains a Damnation Clause that clearly and unequivocally states that my photo "cannot be used in conjunction with any satanic reference, including but not limited to Lucifer, Hades, Old Scratch, Hell, Perdition, Beelzebub, or Honey Boo Boo."

Secondly, jobs don't come from hell. They come from people with money who are willing to pay other people to work for them.

Thirdly, I have worked in both fast food and retail and neither one reminded me of the Netherworld. (Although the Taco Bell drive-through at 2 a.m. does smell vaguely of brimstone and sulfur.)

**None of us expected these jobs to lead to a career, but we did them anyway because we wanted spending money, needed to build a work history, or just plain needed something to do.**

Jobs are different than careers, but when you suggest that one is subordinate to the other, you diminish the value of ordinary work. According to the Work Is Not the Enemy Clause in the DJCC, my image may not be used in conjunction with "any statement or action that disparages the value of hard work, regardless of nature of the job or the amount of compensation involved."

**There's the desperate job, the one we had to take because the price of gas shot up, or we bought a new car and had to make payments on it, or needed to pay college tuition. Maybe it was a second job, or something informal on the side, like fixing up and selling cars.** You make the option of working a second job sound like the problem, not the solution. Under the Personal Responsibility Clause of the DJCC, my image "must not be used in association with any language or expression that attempts to portray hardworking people as helpless victims." The DJCC maintains that meeting one's financial obligations is an act of responsibility, not an act of "desperation."

**And then there's the kind of job we wouldn't take again under any conditions, no matter how desperate or bored we were. The conditions were unpleasant if not dangerous, and the pay didn't make up for it.** I understand that some jobs are beneath you. Specifically, those jobs that you find to be "unpleasant" and "low-paying." Unfortunately, under the Hubris Clause of the DJCC, I am forbidden from endorsing "any third-party comments that could be interpreted as elitist, judgmental, haughty, or condescending."

**We can all agree that jobs falling into this last category aren't worth having.** This one, I'm afraid, is in direct conflict with the "Don't Shoot Yourself in the Foot" clause of the DJCC. You see,

Steve, when your air-conditioner breaks, or your toilet explodes, or termites set up shop in your home, the solution to your problem will almost certainly require people who are willing to do something... "unpleasant." (When you find yourself in need of these people, you'd better hope they haven't read your column.)

**But let's talk about the first two categories of jobs.** OK. Fast-food workers, retail clerks, auto mechanics, car salesman, and part-timers. The "jobs from hell." Let's talk.

**Are they good for the people who work them?** Of course they are.

**Are they good for the economy?** Of course they are.

**Tell us what you think in the poll and comments below.** I did. I voted and then I checked the results. Then I threw up in my mouth. Apparently, most of the respondents see no value in the kind of work you've described. That's a seriously bleak outcome and a blatant violation of all the aforementioned clauses, including the "Glass Half-Empty" restriction of the DJCC, which forbids me from lending my name and likeness to anything "heart-breaking, dismal, grim, pessimistic, soul-deadening, or just plain depressing."

**The Muskegon Chronicle and MLive just finished the second segment in a months-long series of articles about jobs in the Muskegon area. In the most recent segment, we wrote about low-paying jobs and the "shadow" economy of people who hack out a living by mowing lawns, scrounging odd jobs, and anything else that comes their way.** I read it. Nowhere does the writer congratulate anyone for their resourcefulness or self-reliance. Instead, you wrote that "desperate times call for desperate measures," a clear infraction of the "Hyperbole Restriction." According to the DJCC, desperation means selling a kidney to ransom your wife and kids. Desperation is not a $10-an-hour construction job with no benefits, as you suggest. That's just work.

**Not all, but some, employers of low-wage workers give their employees opportunity to advance, we wrote.** I have never seen a job that didn't come with the opportunity for advancement. Union, non-union, high pay, low pay, part-time, full-time, freelance, or salaried. Any worker who consistently shows up an hour early and stays late will quickly become indispensable on any job site. That's still a great truth in the wide world of work. Unfortunately, you didn't mention that. Instead, you implied that a worker's only hope of advancement lies with the employer, another screaming inconsistency with the Personal Responsibility Clause.

**People working odd-jobs or doing day labor for money under the table sometimes do so because it's the only option they have, we wrote.** Agreed. But nowhere do you suggest that having one option is better than having no option. Certainly, these people are struggling, but they have not given up. They have not become wards of the state. They are looking for and in many cases finding a way to get by in a brutal economy. Certainly not ideal, but the Glass Half-Empty Restriction and the Context Clause of the DJCC both prohibit my endorsement of all "one-sided comparisons that fail to illustrate how things could always be much, much worse."

**Some people might take an optimistic view of these jobs.** Of course. Some people still see hard work as something to be respected in all its forms. The point is, fewer people share that view than ever before. The majority of people in your poll voted "no" to every question. They believe that whole categories of jobs are "bad" for the worker and "bad" for society at large. That's a clear infraction of the Work Is Not the Enemy Clause of the DJCC and a radical departure of the attitude I encountered in my previous visits to the great state of Michigan.

**Some people might say the work needs to be done and the workers are filling that need.** I would hope so. Your own paper reported that $2 trillion is being generated by this "shadow economy." That's 8% of our GDP. I'm no economist, but I'd wager an 8% drop in the GDP would start the next Great Depression. And while the *Dirty Jobs* Code of Conduct doesn't address it directly, I'd prefer that my name and likeness avoid any direct association with any type of economic collapse.

**Some will say that nobody forced people to take these jobs. That these jobs enable these people to earn money and pay for things that matter to them. These jobs may mean that individuals are able to rely more on their own earnings and less on taxpayer-funded assistance programs.** Now those people sound more like the Michiganders I remember! The Soo Locks workers in Sault Ste. Marie, the log cabin builders in the U.P., the mobile butchers in Holland, the Bone Black workers in Melvindale, the many good folks on Mackinac Island (in those "hellish" retail and food service positions), the craftsmen at Novadai Furniture right there in Muskegon, and, of course, the maintenance workers on the Mighty Mac. Those people would never look down their noses at an honest day's work. No way.

**Others might take a more negative view. Advocates of living-wage policy might say that low-wage jobs are hurtful to the people working them.** The world is full of well-intentioned people who believe that prices, wages, and rents should should have nothing to do with pesky things like supply and demand. While I applaud their intentions, I'm afraid the Common Sense Clause of the DJCC does not allow my name or likeness to be associated with any views or expressions that could be interpreted as "unrealistic or childlike."

**Some might say that people working in a "shadow economy" are part of the symptoms of an economic system breaking down.** I have no idea if the economy is breaking down or just evolving, but regardless, low-paying, part-time, and off-the-grid jobs are here to stay. We can either talk about these jobs with a measure of dignity and respect, or we can adapt your labeling system of "Bad, Unpleasant, Dangerous, Not-Worth-Having, and Hellish." Honestly, I don't see the point of attacking honest work under any circumstances (although the Futility Clause of the DJCC prohibits me from expecting a cogent reply from those who do).

**A few might even quote the United Nations' Universal Declaration of Human Rights, which states that "Everyone has the right to work, to free choice of employment, to just and favorable conditions of work and to protection against unemployment."** That's very sweet. Unfortunately, the Delusional Thinking Restriction of the DJCC is very clear on this: "under no circumstances will artist's name and likeness be used to declare or proclaim anything that might suggest the endorsement of a utopian or fairy-tale state."

Too bad, really. If it weren't for the Delusional Thinking Restriction, I might very well petition the UN to declare and demand "protection from the ever-widening Skills Gap." According to the Bureau of Labor and Statistics, 3.7 million jobs are currently available that companies can't seem to fill—600,000 positions in manufacturing alone.

All of these jobs pay more than the "living wage." Many provide free training and benefits. None of them are "off the grid." They're available right now to anyone willing to learn a new skill. Unfortunately, no one seems to want them.

**What do you think?** Well, Steve, I'm no expert (and the Hubris Clause of the DJCC forbids me from pretending to be one), but after a lot of careful reflection, I think we might have our head up our ass.

There's a trillion dollars of college debt on the books, and we're still pushing a four-year degree like it's some sort of golden ticket. Dozens of states are facing massive shortages in the skilled trades, but we still talk about trade schools as "alternatives for the academically challenged." And now, with record-high unemployment and Detroit flat broke, you want to focus on the problem of ..."bad jobs"? Can you imagine our grandparents bemoaning the existence of "unpleasant" work? Can you imagine the greatest generation agreeing that some jobs were just "not worth having"?

Look, I don't want to sound like the cranky neighbor on the front porch, screaming at the kids to get off his lawn. (And, yes, the Cranky Neighbor Clause of the DJCC expressly forbids this.) But come on—twelve million people are looking for work and three million jobs can't be filled? How come nobody is asking questions about that? Why is no one taking a poll on whether our expectations have replaced our common sense? Why do we talk only of "job creation," when we can't even fill the jobs we have?

On *Dirty Jobs*, I met hundreds of men and women who found success and happiness by doing the "unpleasant" thing. I remember a guy in Washington whose first job was cleaning the grease trap in a Mexican restaurant. He moved on to washing dishes and then waiting tables. Today, he owns the restaurant and six more just like it. I'd like to read more stories about people like that, and I bet I'm not alone.

Don't get me wrong, I care about the people you write about. For what it's worth, I run a modest foundation that's focused on scholarships for those who are willing to learn a useful skill. But let's not forget about the people who did it the hard way. People who took the jobs you dismissed as "not worth having" and then prospered. People who didn't shy away from the "bad jobs" and ultimately learned to love them. If you ever write a story about them, please feel free to use my image. According to the spirit of the "*Dirty Jobs* Code of Conduct," that's what it's there for.

In the meantime, give my regards to the maintenance men next time you drive over the Mighty Mac. And if the bridge is still standing, tell them I said thanks!

*Best,*
**Mike Rowe**

# THE WORST ADVICE IN THE WORLD

*This is a true story about my high school guidance counselor and the worst advice I ever got (even worse than the "worst advice" I wrote about in Forbes). I wanted you to see it because people are still giving it and, unfortunately, still taking it. The poster in question was recreated and is now sold on profoundlydisconnected.com for $10. Thanks to Brian Huff over at MTI, thousands are now hanging in schools across the country. Which amuses me to no end.*

**WHEN I WAS 17,** my high school guidance counselor tried to talk me into going on to earn a four-year degree. I had nothing against college, but the universities that Mr. Dunbar recommended were expensive, and I had no idea what I wanted to study. I thought a community college made more sense, but Mr. Dunbar said a two-year school was "beneath my potential." He pointed to a poster hanging behind his desk. On one side of the poster was a beaten-down, depressed-looking, blue-collar worker; on the other side was an optimistic college graduate with his eyes on the horizon. Underneath, the text read: "Work Smart NOT Hard."

"Mike, look at these two guys," Mr. Dunbar said. "Which one do you want to be?" I had to read the caption twice. "Work Smart NOT Hard"?

Back then universities were promoting themselves aggressively, and propaganda like this was all over the place. Did it work?

Work Smart NOT Hard
© 1972

# Work Smart ~~NOT~~ AND Hard

Well, it worked for colleges, that's for sure. Enrollments soared. But at the same time, trade schools faltered. Vocational classes began to vanish from high schools. Apprenticeship programs and community colleges became examples of "alternative education," vocational consolation prizes for those who weren't "college material."

Today student loans eclipse $1 trillion. There's high unemployment among recent college graduates, and most graduates with jobs are not even working in their field of study. And we have a Skills Gap. At last count, three million jobs are currently available that either no one can do or no one seems to want. How crazy is that?

I think often about the people I met on *Dirty Jobs*. Most of them were tradesmen. Many were entrepreneurs and innovators. Some were millionaires. People are always surprised to hear that, because we no longer equate dirt with success. But we should.

I remember Bob Combs, a modest pig farmer who fabricated from scratch a massive contraption in his backyard that changed the face of modern recycling in Las Vegas by using the casino food-waste stream to feed his animals. He was offered $75 million for his operation and turned it down. He's a tradesman.

Then there was Matt Freund, a dairy farmer in Connecticut who thought his cows' manure might be more valuable than their milk and who built an ingenious machine that makes biodegradable flowerpots out of cow crap. He now sells millions of Cow Pots all over the world. He's a tradesman.

Mostly, I remember hundreds of men and women who loved their jobs and worked their butts off: welders, mechanics, electricians, plumbers. I've met them in every state and seen firsthand a pride of workmanship that simply doesn't exist in most "cleaner" industries. And I've wondered, why aren't they on a poster? Why aren't we encouraging the benefits of working smart AND hard?

The Skills Gap is bad news for the economy, but it also presents an opportunity. Last month I ran into a woman named Mary Kaye

Cashman who runs a Caterpillar dealership in Las Vegas, and she told me they had more than twenty openings for heavy-equipment technicians. That's kind of astonishing. A heavy-equipment technician with real-world experience can earn upward of six figures. And the training program is free! But still the positions go unfilled? In a state with 9.6 percent unemployment? What's going on?

Here's a theory: What if "Work Smart NOT Hard" is not just a platitude on a poster? What if it's something we actually believe? I know it's a cliché, but clichés are repeated every day by millions of people. Is it possible that a whole generation has taken the worst advice in the world?

Look again at the image on the poster, which I reproduced just the way I remember it. Those stereotypes are still with us. We're still lending billions of dollars we don't have, to kids who can't pay it back, in order to educate them for jobs that no longer exist. We still have three million jobs we can't fill. Maybe it's the legacy of a society that would rather work smart than hard.

Last month I launched an online campaign called "Lessons From the Dirt." It's a modest attempt to get people talking about the skilled trades in a more balanced way. If you're not opposed to a little tasteful vandalism, check out my updated version of Mr Dunbar's poster on ProfoundlyDisconnected.com. The image might amuse you, but the caption is no joke: "Work Smart AND Hard."

I don't know if changing one little word in one stupid slogan will reinvigorate the skilled trades. I just think it's time for a new cliché. My own trade—such as it is—started with an "alternative education," purchased for a reasonable price at a two-year school. I suspect a lot of others could benefit from a similar road. So get a poster and hang it high. And if you see Mr. Dunbar, tell him I turned out OK.

# WHAT MY FATHER TAUGHT ME

*I wrote this on my dad's birthday. It's here in the Appendix because the way we feel about work starts long before the day we get a job. It was first published in* Popular Mechanics, *June 2013.*

**WHEN I WAS 14,** I woke up one Saturday morning to see my father standing at the foot of my bed, sharpening a double-sided ax. "It's time," he said. "Let's go." My father has a tendency to start conversations in the middle. He's also suspicious of anything too modern. Like nouns.

"Time for what?" I said. Knowing the futility of the question before I even asked, I rolled out of bed, pulled on my jeans and work boots, and tried again. "Is it cold out?"

"Invigorating," he replied. "Your mother made oatmeal. Eat it fast."

Outside, the Massey Ferguson tractor idled impatiently as we loaded up the wood cart with ropes and pulleys, jacks and wedges, two chainsaws, and various other weapons of war. My mother added a lunch box to the arsenal, along with a large thermos of coffee. It started to snow. "Try not to kill yourselves," she said. "Dinner's at 6."

I can't even remember how many times my dad and I drove the old tractor down the stone road, through the lower pasture, and deep into the woods to do battle with the Pine, the Maple, the Oak, and the mighty Locust—his personal favorite. ("The hard wood puts up a tough fight, but it burns the best!") The fact that we heated most of the old farmhouse with nothing but a wood stove was a source of great pride for my father and the inspiration for endless witticisms. ("Chop your own wood—it'll warm you twice!")

Finding the right tree and taking it down properly was an undertaking that my father relished. Although there was nothing valuable nearby for the tree to fall on, my father liked to pretend there was. He imagined himself as the contestant on some sort of lumberjack game show, challenged perhaps to drop the tree between a Mercedes and a school bus full of children with inches to spare on either side. With pulleys and ropes and lots of delicate chainsaw work, he would coax the tree to the ground, determined to see it land precisely where he wanted it. ("Measure twice, cut once! That's the ticket, my boy!")

Once the tree was on the ground, we'd strip the limbs and branches and cut them to stove-length pieces. Then we'd turn our attention to the trunk, working backwards from top to bottom. As each cut became progressively thicker, the chainsaw whined louder and higher. ("Sharpen that blade, son. A dull one's twice as dangerous!") I still remember how my arms shook, even after the thing was turned off and put away.

Hauling the wood back to the house was a full day's work. But splitting the larger chunks into pieces that fit the insatiable wood stove—that was a chore without end. Every day after school meant an hour in the woodpile with Dad. I can still hear his voice as I prepared to swing the ax: "Aim for the chopping block, Mike, not the wood. If you aim for the wood you'll hit nothing."

Einstein (being Einstein) was right. Chopping wood yields immediate results, and it's gratifying to see progress unfold. But up there in the woodpile, the real gratification would be delayed. Because my dad was not just teaching me how to swing an ax—he was teaching me that work and play were two sides of the same coin. He was showing me how to enjoy the challenges of doing a hard thing. He was preparing me to become a perpetual apprentice—a role that eventually would define my unlikely career in television.

A few years ago, I stumbled across a poem that I had forgotten about. It's called "Two Tramps in Mud-Time," and it took me back to those days at the woodpile with my dad. In it, Robert Frost is splitting wood in his own backyard, ruminating on work and life. He wrote:

> "My object in living is to unite
> My avocation and my vocation
> As my two eyes make one in sight.
> For only when love and need are one
> And work is play for mortal stakes
> Is the deed ever really done
> For Heaven and for future's sake."

My dad is 80 this year. He no longer ventures into the woods or swings the ax. But the blade is still sharp. And the trees still fall where he wants them.

# SENATE TESTIMONY

*A couple of years ago, I was invited to Washington, D.C., to testify before the Senate Committee on Commerce, Science & Transportation. According to the email, our highest elected officials wanted to hear from a variety of experts about the problems facing America's workforce, with a specific emphasis on infrastructure, manufacturing, vocational education, and the widening Skills Gap.*

*I was flattered, but suspicious. Even though I'd been talking about these issues for years, I had no real qualifications to do so and no reason to believe a roomful of Senators would include me on a panel of noted economists and esteemed business leaders. Plus, my parents live in Maryland, and they are not beyond concocting an elaborate deception to lure me back East under false pretenses. So I RSVP'd with a request to speak directly with the President of the United States. I included my phone number. I also asked if a ball cap would be acceptable attire on the Senate floor.*

*Three days later I heard from an aide who claimed to be calling from Senator Jay D. Rockefeller's office. He wanted a copy of my sworn testimony in advance. "In advance of what?" I asked.*

*"In advance of your appearance here next week," he said.*

*If this was a prank, it was a good one. The caller ID on my phone said U.S. Capitol, and the aide sounded pretty convincing.*

*"Senator Rockefeller is the Chairman of the Senate Commerce Committee," he said. "He needs your sworn testimony on file as soon*

115

*as possible. In writing. We'll provide copies to the press. At the hearing, you'll have exactly five minutes to read your sworn testimony into the public record. Any questions?"*

*I was a little uncomfortable with phrases like "sworn testimony" and "public record." And I still wasn't convinced the aide wasn't really my father doing a funny voice.*

*"Quick," I said. "Who's the Senate Minority Whip?"*

*"Mitch McConnell."*

*"What's Nancy Pelosi's middle name?"*

*"Patricia."*

*"How much is Senator Rockefeller worth these days?"*

*"A lot."*

*He appeared to be legitimate. "Come to the Russell Senate Building next Thursday," he said. "The hearing begins at noon. Don't be late. Wear a tie. And maybe lose the ball cap."*

*"OK," I said. "I'll be there."*

*Long story short, the invitation was legit. I flew to D.C. and told a room full of elected officials why our country's relationship with hard work and skilled labor has devolved into the dysfunctional mess it is today. I told Chairman Rockefeller that many of the work-related challenges we typically describe as problems—a crumbling infrastructure, declining manufacturing, and the widening Skills Gap—are not problems at all, but symptoms of this broken relationship at work. I talked a little bit about education, too, and the fallacy of pushing a four-year degree as the best path for the most people. Mostly, though, I talked about my grandfather.*

**CHAIRMAN ROCKEFELLER,** Ranking Member Hutchison, and members of this committee, my name is Mike Rowe, and I want to thank you very much for the opportunity to share a few thoughts about our country's relationship with manufacturing, hard work, and skilled labor.

I'm here today because of my grandfather.

His name was Carl Knobel, and he was known by most everyone as a jack-of-all-trades. To me, though, he was a magician. For most of his life, my grandfather woke up clean and came home dirty, and the stuff he accomplished in between was nothing short of miraculous.

Somedays he might reshingle a roof. Or rebuild a motor. Or maybe run electricity out to our barn. He was a plumber, a mechanic, a mason, a carpenter, and a master electrician. He built the church I went to as a kid and the farmhouse my brothers and I grew up in. To my knowledge, he never once read the directions to anything. He just knew how stuff worked.

I remember one Saturday morning when I was twelve. I woke up, went to the bathroom, and flushed the toilet the same way I always had. The toilet, however, responded in a way that was completely out of character. There was a rumbling sound, followed by a distant gurgle. Then, everything that had gone down reappeared in a rather violent and spectacular fashion.

Naturally, my grandfather was called in to investigate, and within the hour, we were in the front yard with picks and shovels. By lunch, the lawn was littered with fragments of old pipe, long lengths of new pipe, and mounds of dirt. There was welding. There was pipe-fitting. There were blisters. There was also a lot of banging and laughing, and by sunset, we were filthy. But the new pipe was installed, the dirt was back in the hole, and our toilet was back on its best behavior. It was one of my favorite days ever.

Thirty years later, I was living in San Francisco when my toilet blew up again. This time, I called Roto-Rooter, left a check on the kitchen counter, and went away for a few days. When I got home, the mess was cleaned up and the problem was solved. This time, though, I had no idea who actually solved it, because I never met the guy who did the work. And to be honest, I made no attempt to find out.

It occurred to me that somewhere during those last thirty years, I had become disconnected from a number of things that used to fascinate me. I no longer thought about the person who was growing my food, or the person who was making my clothes, or the person who was making my car. In general, I had become less interested in how things were made and more interested in how things were purchased.

At this point my grandfather was into his nineties, and after a long visit one weekend, I decided on the flight back to San Francisco to do a TV show in his honor. Something simple—a short series of specials that portrayed hard work with humor and relevance. Today, *Dirty Jobs* is still on the air, and I am here before the United States Senate, hoping to say something useful. So here it is.

I think we need to reinvigorate the trades by fostering a heightened sense of appreciation for the people who keep the lights on. In essence, I think we need a national PR campaign for hard work and skilled labor.

If what I'm hearing is true, our manufacturing sector is in decline. Our infrastructure is crumbling. And most puzzling, we are confronted with a widening Skills Gap—even with record-high unemployment. In Alabama, I'm told that 30 percent of the skilled work force is now north of 55 and retiring fast. No one is there to replace them. And Alabama's not alone.

A few months ago in Atlanta, I ran into Tom Vilsack, our Secretary of Agriculture. Tom told me about a recent conversation he had with a governor, who was unable to move forward on the construction of a brand-new power plant. The reason was chilling. It wasn't a lack of funds. It wasn't a lack of support. It was a lack of qualified welders.

In a very general way, I think we've been discouraging the same types of jobs that we've been trying to create. And it seems to me that those jobs would be more appealing to more people, if we all had a greater appreciation for the work itself.

Over the years, a career in the technical trades has become a kind of vocational "consolation prize." We discourage our kids from pursuing those types of jobs. Not because we hate tradesmen, but because we've been conditioned to think of dirty jobs as subordinate to something else—something "better."

Today, my grandfather's skills would be described as "shovel-ready." His knowledge, a product of "alternative education." Show me a plumber on TV, and I'll show you a 300-pound punchline with low-slung pants. What no one talks about is that an hour with a good plumber will soon cost more than an hour with a good psychiatrist. At which point a lot of us will probably be in need of both.

I think skilled labor has an image problem. And I'm here today because guys like my grandfather are no longer seen as a critical part of our workforce. In fact, they're barely seen at all. As a country, we've left our check on the kitchen counter. We are waiting for somebody else to do the work. Somebody we have no relationship with.

Hosting *Dirty Jobs* has given me a rare opportunity to reconnect with these people. But the PR campaign I encourage you to consider is not for the benefit of skilled workers—it's for anyone who shares my addiction to paved roads, smooth runways, reliable bridges, hot water, cool air, and indoor plumbing. It's for parents and kids who might otherwise not consider the vital importance of learning a skill and mastering a trade. It's for everyone.

We need to start promoting the technical trades with the same intensity and scale as we promote a four-year degree. Because there is simply no part of our workforce more critical to making civilized life possible for the rest of us.

# WHAT'S BEHIND THE SKILLS GAP?

*The whole point of Profoundly Disconnected and mikeroweWORKS was to help generate press around the Skills Gap, which I'm happy to say is happening more and more. What follows is a great example of a major publication—*Innovation & Technology Today—*using mikerowe-WORKS to turn a difficult and confusing topic that no one wants to write about into a major cover story with a (relatively) entertaining Q&A with your humble author.*

**IF SOMEONE TOLD YOU THAT,** right now in the good ol' US of A, there are *millions* of good-paying jobs unfilled due to a lack of skilled workers, would you be surprised? Perhaps dumbfounded?

If so, you would not be alone. In an era of 24-hour news cycles dedicated to endless loops of celebrity gossip and "gotcha journalism," the Skills Gap has scarcely been covered by the mainstream media—until now.

*Innovation & Technology Today* has talked with some key players to expose this conundrum, while at the same time exploring solutions in definable terms. The issue not only affects the unemployed, but its cross-sector applicability is directly tied to U.S. economic development.

"We are lending money we don't have to kids who can't pay it back to train them for jobs that no longer exist. That's nuts," said

Mike Rowe of the mikeroweWORKS Foundation. Never before has a complex issue been summarized so succinctly. Rowe, host of the popular Discovery Channel show *Dirty Jobs,* has made it his foundation's mission to help close the country's Skills Gap by challenging the misconceptions that surround "alternative education."

"We've got a trillion dollars in student loans and hundreds of thousands of graduates who can't find work in their chosen field," Rowe said. "Meanwhile, welders and pipe fitters are in short supply all over the country. For people willing to learn a useful skill and work hard, opportunities are everywhere. But the prevailing perceptions are powerful. And changing them takes time."

When asked if this is an attitude of "American Exceptionalism," Rowe was a bit more measured. "That's a bit beyond my pay grade. But I think, in general, most people are programmed to take the path of least resistance," he said. "It's natural for parents to want something for their kids that's better than what they had. The question is, what exactly does 'better' mean in 2013? Is it better to graduate from Georgetown with a law degree, or is it better to know how to repair heavy machinery in North Dakota? I know people in both positions. One is debt-free with a house he paid for in cash and more work than he can ever hope to finish. The other owes $130,000 in student loans, can't find a job, and lives back home in his parents' basement. I think maybe it's less about 'exceptionalism' and more about 'expectationalism.'"

Rowe brings up an interesting point. If there are millions of good-paying tech jobs available right now, and over 80 percent do not require a four-year degree, what is the disconnect? Are young people not inspired by science and math anymore? Is it a lingering negative association with going to a tech school instead of a four-year college? Or is it that these skilled labor jobs have the stigmatic word "labor" associated with them? It seems clear that, in this new economy, work ethic and skill are part of the equation.

According to Mary Kelly, President and CEO of StrataTech Education Group, "Mike Rowe understands the Skills Gap, but he also understands the work ethic. Work ethic is important. When you're talking about welding, yes, they can make a lot of money. We have guys coming out of a seven-month program and making a great living, but some of them are working on a pipeline, in the cold, by themselves, rolling around in the dirt. They are doing 6g welding in a confined space using a mirror to weld. It's hard work! If they don't have that work ethic, they're certainly not going to make that kind of money.

"I think Mike's message is the right message, which is, 'Look, the Skills Gap we need to fix, but we also need to focus on the work ethic, too.'"

In the spirit of putting your money where your mouth is, mikerowe-WORKS has partnered with top technical schools, like those under the StrataTech umbrella, to offer scholarships to students who demonstrate not only academic skills but also pledge work ethic as well—*by signing the pledge.* How's that for old-school principles mixed with high-tech training?

As skilled tradesmen from the baby boomer generation retire in droves, hundreds of thousands of positions are in need of fresh, talented workers. Countless companies have vacancies that can't be filled because of a shortage of skilled workers, which affects the entire economy. We are not just talking about plumbers, welders, and pipe fitters—but also science, technology, engineering, and mathematics, or STEM.

In a famous 2011 conversation, President Obama asked the late Steve Jobs why Apple products could not be made in the U.S. Jobs replied, "Those jobs aren't coming back." Apple took a public relations hit for that statement, but as it turns out, Jobs was right. U.S. workers are simply not as skilled as their overseas counterparts at computer and device engineering.

Larry Bock, serial entrepreneur and biotech investor, believes the answer is to celebrate science. Bock should know. As he started and built new companies in the U.S., he could no longer find homegrown talent to fill those key positions. Bock has a new initiative to end this trend: the USA Science & Engineering Festival, which takes place April 25–27, 2014, in Washington, D.C.

"I wanted to find a way to bring together children, families, scientists, educators, tech companies, government leaders, and celebrities to create an event that celebrated science, and that's how the USA Science & Engineering Festival came together," he said. "It gives kids the tools to change the world.

"Our schools aren't producing the highly trained and highly skilled workers needed. And our young people aren't inspired to pursue these career paths in science, technology, engineering, and math. This is already having repercussions in our economy, and it will only worsen unless we find a way to address it.

"A society gets what it celebrates. If we celebrate the sports stars, musicians, and the Kardashians, they will inspire children down those pathways in life. As a nation, we can do better than that. We need to do better than that," he added.

Who will do the heavy lifting to shift this paradigm? According to Bock, it will need to be a collaboration of government and the private sector. "But perhaps more importantly, it needs to be a collaboration of parents and educators constantly focusing on the STEM fields and constantly inspriring kids to pursue it, particularly young women and children of color," he said.

One organization, Project Lead The Way, is helping to do just that. Project Lead The Way (PLTW) is a 501(c)(3) nonprofit organization and the nation's leading provider of STEM programs. It develops a pipeline of interested, prepared graduates to become the next generation of problem solvers, critical thinkers, collaborators, innovators, and entrepreneurs. PLTW does this through its curriculum, teacher training, and expansive network. It is now in more than 5,200 schools in all 50 states and growing at a rate of more than 20 percent a year.

There is also an organized and growing movement, led by the National Girls Collaborative Project, to help women receive the access and opportunities they need—along with the support of their parents, who are key to providing positive reinforcement. More women tech role models wouldn't hurt, either.

With big names like Mike Rowe, megacorporations like Lockheed Martin, Chevron, and Northrup Grumman and huge festivals like the USA Science & Engineering Festival, it's time for our elected officials to get their acts together. They say attitude is a direct reflection of leadership, and the leadership in Washington has been vapid at best and downright hostile at times when it comes to investing in innovation. How can the richest nation on Earth justify not investing in the three million jobs that can't be filled right here because of the Skills Gap? To those budget hawks always willing and able to slash spending on science, innovation, and education, while feeding pork barrel projects and military programs even the Pentagon doesn't want, we ask, "What do you think will be the real cost of failing to invest in our nation's future?"

The Skills Gap affects five things above all: our young people's sense of purpose and contribution; the ability of our businesses to expand; our economy's ability to grow and prosper; our nation's legacy of innovation; and the American dream itself. Question is, what are we going to do about it?

Hold that thought...*Duck Dynasty* is coming on.

**by *Charles Warner*,** *Publisher*
*Innovation & Technology Today*

*Innovation & Technology Today Q&A: Millions of Americans know Mike Rowe as the* Dirty Jobs *guy, the host of one of the most popular shows in cable TV history. But did you also know he's one of the nation's foremost promoters of finding skilled workers to fill the gaps that exist in technology and other industries? Here's what Mike had to say when we caught up with him:*

**[*Innovation & Technology Today:*] Mike, what was life like for you before *Dirty Jobs?* [*Mike Rowe:*]** I had maybe 300 separate employers. I started in the Baltimore Opera, did some community theater, and appeared in some truly unfortunate infomercials. I also narrated everything with the word "wildebeest" in it. (Trust me, it never works out well for the wildebeest.) My first actual job in TV was on the QVC Shopping Channel. I worked the graveyard shift there for three years and became fairly facile at impersonating a TV host. I was eventually fired in 1993—deservedly—and moved to Hollywood. I've been working on this or that ever since.

**Was a career in television always the plan?** No. God, no. I wanted to be a tradesman. I lived next door to my grandfather—one of those men who just seemed to know how things worked. With no formal education, he went on to master just about every trade. Carpentry, electrical, plumbing, mechanical...the guy could build a house without a blueprint. I wanted to do that.

**What happened?** I didn't get the handy gene. Skipped right over me.

**Bummer.** Tell me about it. In high school, I washed out of every shop class there was. I had no aptitude for the thing I wanted to do and couldn't understand why I was failing.

**What did you do?** I let it go. I enrolled at a community college and took some random courses in a bunch of things I had never considered. Philosophy. Rhetorical analysis. Speech. I learned to sing. I learned to write. I learned to act. I joined the debate team. I guess I left the industrial arts for the liberal arts, but when I started working for a living, I still thought of myself as a tradesman. I still do. With a slightly different tool box.

**So how do you explain *Dirty Jobs?* You shot for eight years in all 50 states. For a guy with commitment issues, that was a pretty big bite.** Total miscalculation. I was pitching an idea called *Somebody's Gotta Do It,* a short-term project about real people doing real work that I thought my grandfather might enjoy watching. Discovery called it a "talk show in a sewer," but agreed to order three hours. They changed the name to *Dirty Jobs* and gave me a budget that rivaled my first weekly allowance. In turn, I signed some paperwork that gave them the right to order more episodes, if by some unthinkable chance people actually watched. Eight years later, we were still shooting. Careful what you wish for....

**So your whole business model evaporated overnight?** Yeah. Along with my attitude. *Dirty Jobs* was personal, and when it went to series, I was determined to keep it that way. No writers, no actors, no scripts, no "confessionals," and no second takes. Nothing fake. It was hard work for sure—we were on the road 300 nights a year. But it was simple and honest. And a hell of a lot of fun.

**Yet, for all its humor and simplicity, *Dirty Jobs* touched on some very big themes. Entrepreneurship, innovation, the dignity of work, the definition of a "good job."** Those themes were always in the show, but they didn't really become central until the economy crashed. In 2008, unemployment was headline news, and there was constant talk about how "all the good jobs had vanished." But *Dirty Jobs* was telling another story. Every week, we proved that lots of jobs still exist for people who are willing to learn a useful skill and work their butts off. Reporters were suddenly interested in a "*Dirty Jobs* perspective." I was happy to share it.

**During that time, on Labor Day 2008, you started mikerowe-WORKS. You called it a PR campaign for skilled labor and alternative education.** Right. It was also an online Trade Resource Center, built by fans of the show. We assembled thousands of apprenticeship programs and on-the-job training opportunities and posted them in one place. I started to publicly challenge the narrative that high unemployment means no jobs and that a good education can only come with a four-year degree.

**You also challenge the stigmas and stereotypes associated with skilled labor in a very direct way. Why?** Because I don't think the Skills Gap is a problem; I think it's a symptom of what we value. And somewhere along the way, we've stopped valuing hard work and skilled labor. How else can you explain the availability of so many jobs that no one seems to want? If we want to encourage people to get trained for the jobs that actually exist, we have to change the way we talk about work and education. We have to treat the cause, not the symptom.

**The symptoms are pretty scary. Right now, there are three million good-paying jobs that can't be filled in the U.S.** Right. And the crazy thing is, less than 12 percent of those jobs require a four-year degree. Most require specific training and a useful skill.

**So why aren't students considering tech schools as a viable career path?** Because we've spent the last 40 years telling them that tech schools are institutions for functioning idiots. We've spent decades pushing "higher education" to the point that anything less than a diploma now feels like a vocational consolation prize. It's just so damn dysfunctional. We've got a trillion dollars in student loans and hundreds of thousands of graduates who can't find work in their chosen field. Meanwhile, welders and pipe fitters are in short supply all over the country. For people willing to learn a useful skill and work hard, opportunities are everywhere. But the prevailing perceptions are powerful. And changing them takes time.

**What's the next step to close that Skills Gap? Who has to start doing some heavy lifting now that awareness has been created?** We've got to start by rewarding the behavior we want to encourage. At mikeroweWORKS, we offer work ethic scholarships. They're a bit controversial, but they get people talking. We're building an association of excellent trade schools around the country. Midwest Technical, Tulsa Welding, Delta Technical, and RSI—they all understand the challenge, and we're working closely with them. I also think companies can do a better job of recruiting, by emphasizing the role of skill wherever it applies. Hundreds of STEM jobs, for instance, require the mastery of a useful skill. And conversely, many skilled jobs require an understanding of STEM. But it's rare to see a welder portrayed as a person who understands the science or mathematical aspects of the work or an engineer with muddy boots, holding a welding torch.

**We understood you'll be at the Science & Engineering Festival in D.C. this April. This is a pretty big deal.** It's a huge deal. They expect a minimum of 250,000 people and tons of press. I'm giving speeches and moderating panels. I've also agreed to host the mikeroweWORKS Pavilion. I'm filling it with dozens of companies that want to show off the relationship between skill and technology in their own businesses. Caterpillar, for instance, will have a huge presence, because they have literally hundreds of positions all over the country for heavy equipment technicians. These jobs are a perfect example of what I'm talking about—they start around $50K, offer free training, and a real chance to make six figures in just a few years. And yet the positions go unfilled. It's baffling.

**Who else would you like to see in your Pavilion?** Any company that relies on a skilled workforce is welcome, especially those with open positions. Turner Construction will be there, along with UTI and some of the schools I just mentioned. Organizations like Go Build Alabama and Skills USA will be there and some companies I worked with on *Dirty Jobs*. Fair Oaks Farms, for instance, is one of the most innovative and successful dairies in the country. Like much of the agricultural industry, they're constantly fighting against the *Hee Haw* stereotypes that plague the modern famer. They'll be showing off all kinds of innovation that's going to blow people away. Also, TechShop, an amazing company combining skill and innovation in a way that's going to impact everyone. I've got calls out to businesses large and small and 12,000 square feet to fill....

**Speaking of innovation and technology, what excites you?** The role that innovation and technology play in the workforce. That's a huge conversation. Obviously, innovation is critically important, but when it exceeds our ability to implement, we get problems. New advancements lead to new efficiencies, new efficiencies lead to smaller workforces, and smaller workforces lead to millions of people sitting around and waiting for someone to create a new job for them. Hence the Skills Gap. Innovation is no good without a national commitment to constantly retrain and reexamine the nature of work and entrepreneurship. This is where our reach has exceeded our grasp. Technology has allowed us to advance faster than we can adapt.

**The U.S. used to manufacture a lot of things, and increasingly, these jobs are being shipped overseas. Are those jobs gone for good?** A lot of companies are trying to retool in the States. But it's tough. I talked to an executive at Walmart the other day and confirmed a story I read about their commitment to put $50 billion of American-made products back on their shelves over the next ten years. That'll require a huge investment in new factories and manufacturing facilities. But the biggest challenge? A skilled and willing workforce. At the moment, there's something like half a million jobs available in manufacturing that companies can't fill. It's not enough to just build factories and run want ads. The workforce needs to be there. Massive training will need to occur. And most of all, people will need to feel excited by the prospect of learning a new skill.

# IN DEFENSE OF BILL

*It's almost impossible to remain nonpartisan around the topic of work, but I try hard to stay impartial. To that end, I've appeared on every network and talked about the Skills Gap with just about every anchor and pundit on TV. But no matter where I go, people get angry if I sit next to the "wrong guy." Here's a reply to a disappointed fan on my Facebook page that didn't approve of my proximity to Bill Maher. It went viral.*

> **Bob R.:** *Mike—Saw you hangin' with Bill Maher. I had no idea you were a liberal. Really blew me away. Love everything you do, but now that I know who you really are, I won't be tuning in to watch anything you're involved with.*

**WELL, HI THERE, BOB**. How's it going? Since your comment is not the only one of its kind, I thought I'd take a moment to address it.

Bill Maher is opinionated, polarizing, and controversial. I get it. So is Bill O'Reilly, which is probably why I heard the same comments after I did his show. ("How could you, Mike? How could you?")

Truth is, every time I go on Fox, my liberal friends squeal. And every time I show up on MSNBC, my conservative pals whine. Not because they disagree with my position—everyone agrees that

closing the Skills Gap is something that needs to happen. No, these days, people get bent simply if I appear on shows they don't like or sit too close to people they don't care for.

What's up with that? Is our country so divided that my mere proximity to the "other side" prompts otherwise sensible adults to scoop up their marbles and go home?

Back in 2008, I wrote an open letter to President Obama, offering to help him promote those three million "shovel-ready" jobs he promised to create during his campaign. (I suspected they might be a tough sell, given our country's current relationship with the shovel.) Within hours, hundreds of conservatives accused me of "engaging with a socialist" and threatened to stop watching *Dirty Jobs with Mike Rowe* if I didn't come to my senses.

When I made the same offer to Mitt Romney (who actually responded), thousands of liberals chastised me for "engaging with a greedy capitalist" and threatened to stop watching *Dirty Jobs* if I didn't take it back.

You may ask, "But what did these people think about the issue at hand?" Who knows? They were too busy being outraged by my proximity to the devil. (Poor Ed Schultz at MSNBC nearly burst into tears. "You were on the wrong stage, Mike! The wrong stage!! With the wrong candidate!!!")

Oy.

Here's the thing, Bob—Profoundly Disconnected is not a PR campaign for Mike Rowe. It's a PR campaign for skilled labor and alternative education. PR campaigns need—that's right—PR, and if I limit my appearances to those shows that I personally watch, hosted only by those personalities with whom I personally agree, I might as well start a church and preach to the choir.

Point is, I didn't go on *Real Time* to endorse B.M., and I didn't go on the *Factor* to endorse B.O. I went on because millions of people watch those shows. I approached our liberal president for the same reason.

Likewise, his conservative opponent. And I showed up on *Sesame Street* with the same agenda that I took to Congress.

Closing the Skills Gap is bigger than you or me or any particular venue, and *Real Time* gave me an opportunity to reach five million people. I'm grateful for that, and I'll do it again if they want me back.

As for Bill Maher off-camera, you'll be pleased to know that the guy was a perfect gentleman. His staff is excellent, and his after-party included an open bar with a spread I've never seen in such a setting. Bill took the time to hang out with his guests and their friends after the show, chatting about this and that for over an hour, and taking pictures with anyone who wanted one. Trust me, that's rare.

Yes, he's outrageous, inflammatory, and, to many, a jagged little pill. But he's also gracious, generous, engaging, and taller than he appears on TV. Which, frankly, surprised me.

— *Mike*

# IN DEFENSE OF GLENN

*After Bill Maher, I was invited to appear on* TheBlaze *with Glenn Beck. Naturally, I went. Naturally, people freaked out. Shannon W. had this to say:*

> **Shannon W.:** *Mike—How could you associate with such a horrible and psychotic person that is Glenn Beck? I wouldn't accept a dime off that hateful, nasty racist. Very disappointed to see this post.*

*An honest question deserves an honest reply....*

**WELL, HI THERE, SHANNON**—and a pleasant good morning to you, too! If you want a detailed answer to your question, please take a moment to read my earlier reply to Bob R., another crestfallen soul who couldn't reconcile my association with a TV host that he personally despised. As you read it (out loud, if possible, and in a public place), kindly replace the words "Bob R." with "Shannon W." and "Bill Maher" with "Glenn Beck." But prepare yourself—you might be forced to conclude that my true objective here has little to do with winning or losing your approval.

As for your personal characterization of Glenn Beck, I can only assume you have information not available to me. In my time with

him, I saw nothing "horrible, psychotic, hateful, or nasty." I smelled no burning sulfur, no smoldering brimstone, and saw no sign of cloven hooves.

To the contrary, I found a very passionate guy who employs about 300 people, works his butt off, and puts his money where his mouth is. Do we agree on everything? Of course not. Am I "disappointed" by that fact? Not at all. The real question, Shannon, is...why are you?

To be clear, I'm not here to tell you what to think or whom to hate. Like everyone else, you're free to pick your devils, choose your angels, and attach the horns and halos accordingly.

But the guts of your question—even without all the name-calling and acrimony—reveal the essence of what's broken in our country. You want to know "how I can associate" with someone you don't like? The short answer is, how can I not? How are we ever going to accomplish anything in this incredibly divisive time if we associate only with people that we don't disagree with?

*— Mike*

**P.S.** Not only did Glenn hand me a check for $25,000 made out to the mikeroweWORKS scholarship fund, he invited me to shoot a few PSAs on his set and offered to air them on his network for free. You know how many other networks have offered to do that? Not one. In addition, his viewers have purchased hundreds and hundreds of "Work Smart AND Hard" posters. I'm already getting photos of them hanging in high schools across the country. Glenn also signed one and took some artistic license on my face. Which made me laugh. We'll auction that off on a future episode of C.R.A.P., and my guess is we'll raise a pretty penny.

**P.P.S.** — Penn Jillette is an avowed atheist. Glenn Beck is a deeply religious Christian. They disagree on a lot, but speak often on

Glenn's show and have some of the most respectful and interesting exchanges on television today.

I've been on every network over the years, more than once, and I'll promise you this—if you want the potential for a thoughtful exchange that's not crammed into a five-minute segment, your options are limited.

# CNN VIEWER HAS QUESTIONS

*I'm a little late to the whole social media thing, but I have to confess, engaging people on this topic is fun and a great way to keep the conversation moving. After an appearance on* Piers Morgan Live, *I heard from Jennifer B. Then, Jennifer B. heard from me.*

**TODAY'S QUESTION** comes from Jennifer B. Jennifer posted over at CNN.com, but I'm answering here because...well, because I need more room.

*[Jennifer B.:]* **How can the middle class send their kids to college for "four or more years" when the Republicans have made it far too expensive with raising interest rates on school loans and wanting to end federal grants?** *[Mike Rowe:]* Your question implies that the middle class should be borrowing money to send their kids to an expensive four-year college. You also imply that college is far too expensive because interest rates on student loans are too high. Might I respectfully challenge both implications?

I understand that, since 1985, college tuition has increased by nearly 500 percent. Can you imagine the same jump in any other area? Food, housing, medicine, energy? If everything we need to live increased in price at the same rate as college tuition, there would

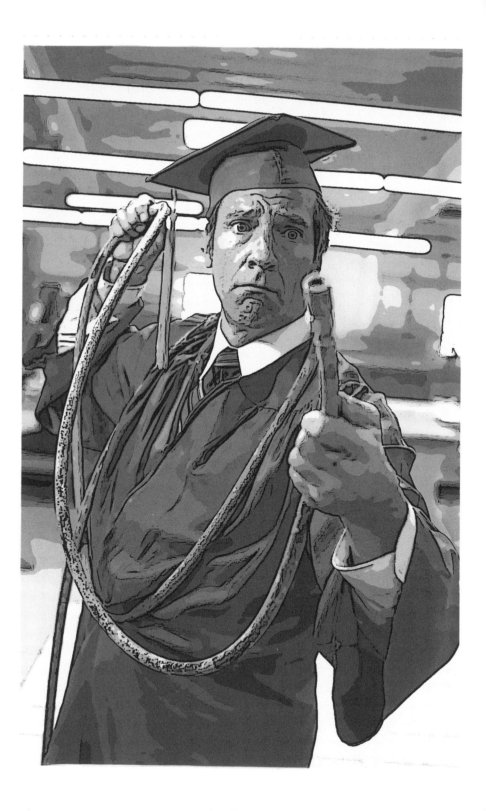

be a national riot in about ten minutes. So what really happened in the marketplace to allow college to get so expensive? Is it really all because Republicans want to raise the rates on student loans?

Think about it. Universities get to decide how much money to charge their students. Likewise, parents and students decide if they can afford to pay it. It's a pretty simple proposition. But when the government suddenly makes hundreds of billions of dollars in student loans readily available—under the popular (and voter-friendly) theory that "everyone should go to college"—we see an unintended consequence. We see colleges suddenly motivated to charge more money. A lot more. And so they embark on their own PR campaigns to boost enrollment. They hire advertising agencies and publicists and lobbyists and go about the business of persuading people to "invest in their future." And most importantly, they provide an admissions department to help arrange for an affordable student loan. This is what's been happening for the last forty years.

If blame is your thing, there's plenty to go around. Republicans and Democrats have both allowed a trillion dollars of public money to flow freely between students and colleges with no real accountability for the results. And millions of well-intentioned parents and guidance counselors are still pushing the idea that a four year degree is the only viable path to happiness. This in spite of the fact that the vast majority of available jobs no longer require a diploma— they require the willingness to learn a useful skill. And that kind of training does not demand the type of massive borrowing that has put college graduates a trillion dollars in the hole.

To be clear, I'm not anti-college; I'm anti-debt. If you can afford it, by all means go for it. But I reject the idea that a four-year school is the best path for the most people. I went on *Piers Morgan Live* because I have a scholarship fund that trains people for jobs that actually exist, while rewarding the kind of work ethic I think we need to encourage. I want to spread the word.

**Vocational training has been taken out of most high schools. Would you not agree that they need to be brought back and kids be given the equivalent of a two-year certification to apply to a trade school: carpentry, welding, electrician...?** Of course. The current Skills Gap has unfolded in part because vocational education vanished from high schools. I'm all for reinstating those programs, but I'm afraid that won't be enough. There are hundreds of thousands of jobs available right now that people simply do not want. This is not because the jobs are "bad" or the pay is lousy. It's because we've raised an entire generation to view these opportunities as subordinate to a four-year degree. Good jobs are going begging because hard work and skilled labor are no longer valued in the same way as they were fifty years ago.

**Do you realize how many jobs would be available if greedy corporations kept manufacturing and technical jobs here?** Yes, I think I do. But what makes you think they would be filled?

Consider this: Right now, in the manufacturing sector alone, 600,000 jobs are currently available. That's 600,000 open positions that American manufacturers can't fill. You're right—if all the American corporations moved all their manufacturing facilities and factories back to the United States, we'd have a few million more openings. But then what? Do you really assume that millions of unemployed Americans would run to fill those positions? I'm afraid it's not that simple. If it were, it would already be happening. We wouldn't have a Skills Gap. But we do, and it's getting wider every year. The fact is—according to the government's own numbers— 3.7 million jobs are available right now. Doesn't it make sense to fill those positions before we start demanding that companies create more opportunities that people don't aspire to?

Like it or not, we're in a global economy, and it's not the politicians or the corporations calling the shots. It's us. What we do as consumers matters far more than what we say as citizens. Right now, for instance, I'll wager you're reading this on a device made in China. It's not a criticism—just an observation. Every single thing in our world, from Honey Boo Boo to your iPhone to your local Congress person is a reflection of the things we value and the choices we make. At the cash register and at the polls.

**The list goes on, but I would say to you that the GOP won't even pass the Jobs Bill and does nothing to help the middle class and our active military or veterans.** Yes, Jennifer, your list does go on. And on the other side of the aisle there is another American with a different list. And their list goes on as well. This is the problem. Everyone is so focused on making their own list and keeping track of how screwed up the other side is, they can't acknowledge a good idea unless somebody on their side tells them how to feel about it. Funny thing is, most of the Republicans I know want the same basic things as most of the Democrats I know. They all want more jobs. They all want a healthy planet. They all support our veterans. And they all want to help people who are in genuine need of help. But they disagree on the method and on the role of government. And because they can't get past their methodology, they just keep adding more things onto their list. And so it goes.

**They talked jobs, jobs, jobs, and all they've done is help their rich cronies, obstruct job-making bills, make higher education unaffordable for everyone BUT their rich supporters!!** I get it. The Republicans are bad. (I know this because you have used both CAPS and exclamation points!!) You have identified the GOP and their rich friends as the cause of a great many problems. You are certainly not alone. But frankly, I don't find your analysis to be all that persuasive. For one thing, millions of conservatives are far from rich. And millions of liberals are far from poor. Does the government have a huge role to play? Sure. But ultimately, the way out of this is not through D.C. The buck no longer stops there. It stops with us. It has to.

**Why don't you look at THOSE facts and ask the GOP to get off their collective derrières, help create jobs and quit jeopardizing the future of the American people?!** Because honestly, Jennifer, I don't believe that the GOP or the Dems or the president can actually "create" jobs. The best they can do is encourage an environment where people who might be willing to assume the risk of hiring other people are more inclined to do so. That's what I'd like them to do. And to the extent that either party would ever listen to a guy that used to have a show on cable TV—that's about all I would ask of them.

**By the way, people WILL work their butt off, Mike, if paid a fair living wage and have affordable health care.** From what I've seen of the world, most people (including me), would rather work eight hours instead of ten, six hours instead of eight, four hours instead of six. Most people prefer more vacation time than less. Most people want their gratification as soon as possible. Given a choice, most people would rather be comfortable than uncomfortable.

Again, this is not a criticism—it's just the human condition. As a society, we can either encourage or discourage this basic tendency. In a very general way, I think we've encouraged it. I think we've encouraged people to withhold their very best efforts and their very hardest work until certain conditions and expectations are met. And I think those conditions are both relative and ever-changing. So when you suggest that people won't work their butts off unless or until they feel that they are fairly paid and provided with affordable health care, I think you're absolutely right. That's exactly where our expectations have brought us.

On *Dirty Jobs with Mike Rowe,* though, I got a chance to meet a different breed. I met hundreds of men and women who proved beyond all doubt that hard work didn't necessarily have to be conditioned on anything other than a personal decision to bust your own ass. By and large, the workers I met on that show were happy and successful because they were willing to work harder than everyone else around them. And in doing so, they thrived. Not right away, perhaps, but over time most of them prospered. They distinguished themselves on the job by outworking the competition. And they advanced. In fact, many of the "Dirty Jobbers" we featured were millionaires. You just wouldn't know it because they were usually covered in grime or sludge or shit or something worse. During the show, I also spoke at length with employers in every state and in every industry. And no matter where I went, the biggest challenge was always the same—finding people who were willing to learn a new skill and work hard. I hear the same thing today.

Last week, I spent a few hours with the head of labor relations for one of the largest engineering firms in the world. He has thousands of positions open right now. Literally thousands. After Katrina, his firm poured many millions of dollars into workforce development down in the Gulf. They trained—for free—hundreds of workers in a variety of positions that offered all kinds of opportunities to advance. The pay was fair. The benefits were solid. But the program ultimately failed. Why? Because virtually every single trainee decided it was just too damn hot. I'm not even kidding. They just didn't want to work in the heat. And so—they didn't.

In the next few years, this company anticipates 15,000 new openings for welders and pipe fitters in the Southeast. And the head of recruitment has absolutely no idea where the workers will come from. That should scare us all.

**Getting their hands dirty isn't the problem. Being paid minimum wage with no health care IS the problem!** But, Jennifer, how then do you explain the Skills Gap? These are not "minimum-wage jobs." These are not "jobs with no health care." Again, you seem to assume that any time that a job becomes available that meets your criteria, a qualified and willing candidate will swoop in to fill it. But why do you think that? All the evidence suggests the opposite is true. Three and a half million jobs are available right now. As in—today. What's up with that?

If you tell me the pay is not sufficient, I'll respectfully disagree. I've personally seen thousands of jobs go begging that start around $55,000 and offer a straight path to a six-figure salary. If you tell me it's due to a lack of training, I'll respectfully disagree some more. I haven't seen one training program or trade school in the country that's maxed out. Not one. I started mikeroweWORKS because I've personally met with dozens of employers who have hundreds of opportunities they can't fill. Not only do these positions offer health care and fair pay, many offer free training. The catch? The work requires real, actual skill, and the conditions are often...uncomfortable. Sometimes it's hot. Sometimes it's cold. But the opportunities are there and include the criteria you want. And yet, companies can't fill them.

Every month, the trade schools I work with tell me about companies that are desperate for more welders. They simply can't train them fast enough. Tulsa Welding School, Midwest Technical, The Refrigeration School, UTI...believe me, there is no shortage of training. No, the Skills Gap reflects more than a lack of ability or a lack of opportunity—it reflects a disconnect between what we want, what we study, what we can afford, and what's actually available.

Last point: Two weeks ago, I talked with a heavy equipment technician up in Butler, North Dakota. Jack is 26 years old. Started welding part-time in high school. Got a job at the local Cat dealer working on big machines. Had a knack for it. Took a training program. Started around $65,000 with a 25 percent "Impact Signing Bonus." Went to work in earnest. Sixty-hour weeks, mostly outside. Tough work, but he was good at it and willing. Doubled his pay in a year. Met a girl. Got married. Bought a house. Had a kid. Got a raise. Paid off his house. Had another kid. Just quit his job to freelance. Why? Because he has a trade that's in demand and real-world experience. He can work when he wants at $150 an hour anywhere on the High Plains. Jack is debt-free, highly trained, good at what he does, and absolutely thriving. Why? Because he combined a useful skill with a solid work ethic and welcomed a chance to be uncomfortable.

A few months ago I wrote something called the S.W.E.A.T. Pledge. It stands for "Skills and Work Ethic Aren't Taboo." (So sue me—I like acronyms.) All mikeroweWORKS scholarships require the recipient to sign this pledge—among other things—before we spend $15,000 to $20,000 training them. If I were a betting man, Jennifer, I'd wager that you will not approve of this 12-point promise. But maybe I'm wrong? Give it a read; tell me what you think. And thanks for the questions.

Happy Sunday,
*Mike*

# IN CASE YOU
# HAVEN'T SEEN IT...

# THE "S.W.E.A.T." PLEDGE
## (Skill & Work Ethic Aren't Taboo)

1. I believe that I have won the greatest lottery of all time. I am alive. I walk the Earth. I live in America. Above all things, I am grateful.

2. I believe that I am entitled to life, liberty and the pursuit of happiness. Nothing more. I also understand that "happiness" and the "pursuit of happiness" are not the same thing.

3. I believe there is no such thing as a "bad job." I believe that all jobs are opportunities, and it's up to me to make the best of them.

4. I do not "follow my passion." I bring it with me. I believe that any job can be done with passion and enthusiasm.

5. I deplore debt and do all I can to avoid it. I would rather live in a tent and eat beans than borrow money to pay for a lifestyle I can't afford.

6. I believe that my safety is my responsibility. I understand that being in "compliance" does not necessarily mean I'm out of danger.

7. I believe the best way to distinguish myself at work is to show up early, stay late and cheerfully volunteer for every crappy task there is.

8. I believe the most annoying sounds in the world are whining and complaining. I will never make them. If I am unhappy in my work, I will either find a new job or find a way to be happy.

9. I believe that my education is my responsibility and absolutely crucial to my success. I am resolved to learn as much as I can from whatever source is available to me. I will never stop learning and understand that library cards are free.

10. I believe that I am a product of my choices—not my circumstances. I will never blame anyone for my shortcomings or the challenges I face. And I will never accept the credit for something I didn't do.

11. I understand the world is not fair and I'm OK with that. I do not resent the success of others.

12. I believe that all people are created equal. I also believe that all people make choices. Some choose to be lazy. Some choose to sleep in. I choose to work my butt off.

On my honor, I hereby affirm the above statements to be an accurate summation of my personal worldview. I promise to live by them.

Signed: _____    Dated: _____

Signed: *Mike Rowe*    Dated: September 2, 2013

www.mikeroweworks.com

# MORE ACKNOWLEDGEMENTS

*Everyone at Simantel,* especially Jake. Simantel is a fine advertising agency full of creative people and clever individuals. But without Jake Beyhl, I wouldn't have anyone to torture with my schizophrenic ideas and complete disregard for manufactured deadlines. Jake embodies the very definition of "creative passion," literally. And he has the tattoos to prove it.

*Everyone on my crew,* especially Barsky. Those of you that watched *Dirty Jobs* will remember Barsky as the cranky and pedantic producer who tried with varying degrees of success to keep the train on the rails. I'll remember him as the only person to care about the show as much as me.

*Everyone at Pilgrim Films and Television,* but especially Craig Piligian. For nearly a year, I tried and failed to sell my idea to every single television channel out there. *Dirty Jobs* was too funny for PBS, but not funny enough for Comedy Central. Too gross for ABC, but not gross enough for Fox. Too smart for NBC, but not smart enough for Nat Geo. And so on. When I pitched it to Discovery, they called it "a talk show in a sewer" and said no thanks. Somehow, Craig talked them into it. I don't know how he did it. I'm not sure I want to know.

*Everyone at Discovery,* especially John. Aside from creating the most trusted name in nonfiction entertainment, John Hendricks is an entrepreneur without equal. He also mentions me in a very flattering way in his new book, *A Curious Discovery,* an excellent read packed with multiple pages filled with actual writing. Additionally, he lets me fly in his private jet once in a while, which I enjoy immensely.

**_Everyone at Midwest Technical Institute, Universal Technical Institute, Tulsa Welding School, and The Refrigeration School,_** especially Brian Huff. Currently, mikeroweWORKS is organizing an association of trade schools with outstanding placement results, and these schools are already onboard. Our goal is to promote their extraordinary results through a scholarship program that rewards work ethic. As of the publication date, nearly $3 million in work ethic scholarships are in the process of being awarded. That's just the beginning, and it all started with a welder named Brian Huff who has a lot of big ideas and the overwhelming desire to share them.

**_Everyone at Evening Magazine,_** especially Mike Orkin and James Reid. Back in 2002, _Evening_ was known for heartwarming stories about food banks, rainbows, quirky collectors, and three-legged dogs. We made it about sewers and slaughterhouses. Mike put "Somebody's Gotta Do It" on the air, which no other executive producer in his right mind would have allowed. And James produced the segments that snapped our narcoleptic audience out of their stupor, horrified CBS corporate, and reinvigorated my own career. True, we all got fired and the show got canceled, but, hey—nothing lasts forever.

**_Everyone in Baltimore,_** especially my mother. Peggy Rowe is a world-class copy editor and a prescient critic of the written word. While she doesn't approve of every sentence in this manuscript, and looks slightly askance at the "gimmicky nature of a one-page book," her unconditional support and encouragement in all things remains unexampled. If she ever decides to write a book of her own, she will almost certainly be hailed as the next Erma Bombeck. Of course, if that should that ever come to pass, I must insist on writing the foreword.

Thanks to everyone who took the photos in this
fake book, but especially Michael Segal. Michael is a
world-class photographer with a soft spot for the skilled
trades. He's generous with his time, fun to work with,
and never asks me to "smile" if I don't feel like it.